First Edition

Smart English:

Discussion Questions & Activities

– China

Student Book: Part 1

Intermediate

Andy Smart

Smart English: TEFL Discussion Questions and Activities – China
Student Book Part 1

ISBN 978-0-9926912-1-9

First Edition published by Andy Smart 2015

About the Author

England

Born in the UK, Andy Smart has been a qualified teacher since obtaining his PGCE at the University of Brighton in 1990 and has been involved in education ever since. In England he taught at secondary school level for many years and was also strongly connected to work with SEN students including those with severe learning difficulties. This focused on integrating them into mainstream classroom activities in order to achieve their GCSE's and 'A' levels. Later, this commitment led to the establishment of a new day centre and an accompanying curriculum for people with autism. Moving to management in further education, his primary role was in finding placements to meet SEN students' individual requirements as well as setting up and running various outreach projects.

From there Andy's involvement shifted to supporting EBD students who had been excluded from school. His work aimed at guiding young people back onto a pathway, safe from the negative influences of modern society. During this period, his team successfully created a specialised centre for their students' education, fostering the skills needed to survive in the outside world.

Asia

In 2005 Andy relocated to China where he began teaching English to adults in the city of Guilin, Guanxi Autonomous Region. From there he moved to South Korea working in Seoul, teaching young people at academies and also giving private tuition to teenagers in their homes. Returning to China in 2007 he started work in Beijing creating a strong network throughout the city. Since then he has been primarily involved in teaching his spoken English lessons, delivering lectures and training.

In many ways this book is a culmination of years of practice in the classroom. Drawing from a diverse background in education and extensive practice during his time in Asia, Andy has been able to develop a successful learning package aimed at people who want to improve their oral English skills. This is a strong and effective system that promotes fluency, confidence and accuracy, building a platform where the learner comes away with a high level of self-achievement. Students therefore start to perceive English in a different manner, instead regarding it as a natural part of their daily life rather than a separate entity that is an ongoing struggle

Contents

Appendixes

Appendix A. Grammar at a Glance

Appendix B. Using Phonetics

Preface

Five Types of Student

As a teacher of spoken English, I never quite know who will come into my classroom. It could be someone who has a low English speaking level and is as quiet as a mouse or someone who is both fluent and confident but realises that they are speaking too formally.

One time I was shocked to see one of our most well known IELTS teachers come into the classroom, then sit down with the other students. He had been with our company for many years and his classes were very popular as were his speeches and lectures.

"Why on earth have you come to my class?" I asked feeling puzzled.
"I need to improve my spoken English" he exclaimed.
"You are joking" I laughed. "Really? Your English is great!"
"Yes, but I need to retake my IELTS. My score was too low, so I have to work harder."
"But you're an IELTS teacher. Surely your score was good enough the first time?"
"No, I only got a 7.5 last time" he replied with an unhappy look.
The other students were all astonished at this remark.
"So what score do you need?" I quizzed with great curiosity.
"I need an 8…………….I have to get into Cambridge!"

It just proves that no matter how good you are, you still need to learn to speak more like a native English speaker to really improve. It's a huge advantage in any IELTS or TOEFL exam and is why more and more people are realising that you can't speak proper English if you only learn from a text book. It's one of the big reasons why so many people come to my classes and why these days, learning spoken English is now so popular in China.

Five Types of Student

There are five types of student who can use the Smart English package:

- Students who are doing an IELTS, TOEFL or other English exams. If you are about to do one of these tests then it is essential that you practice your speaking in order to get the score you need. In these lessons you will focus on fluency, pronunciation, grammar and increasing your vocabulary. You will also learn to speak with a higher degree of confidence and freedom from any set models or ideal answers that many text books provide. Remember an examiner can easily spot a candidate reciting. If they do they may choose to ask a follow-up question which will be much harder. It's much better to learn how to answer questions naturally than trying to remember set questions.

- Professionals who need to improve their speaking skills for work. To many professional people, speaking is not just a matter of learning business English. Of course this is an important aspect of communication but in my experience, most just really want to speak to their foreign clients with confidence and accuracy. Many professionals can feel very self-conscious and embarrassed when talking to native English speakers, especially in meetings and on conference calls.

- People who like learning English out of interest. I often get people who come to class purely for their love of the English language. Their main aim is to make English a part of their life becoming 'second nature'. These people have no pressure and no stress and for all, the Smart English package is an extremely agreeable, interesting and fun way to improve.

- People who are going abroad. For anyone who is leaving China to foreign lands, the use of text book English will not be enough to understand what the real native English speakers are saying. Smart English helps the traveller understand informal language and also cultural aspects of where they are going, especially in real life situations such as eating in restaurants or shopping.

- Chinese English teachers who want to move away from a text book model. I have had many IELTS, TOEFL and other traditional English teachers come to class who realise that the formal way Chinese people are taught English in school is only 50% of how to really speak English properly. To these professionals this offers a new dimension and freedom to how their speaking and how they are perceived by both students and colleagues.

Introduction

Learning to Speak Great Spoken English

It's always fantastic when you get positive feedback, so when one of my students came up to me and said

"Andy, why do we love your classes so much?"

I felt fantastic for the rest of the day. You can't beat praise to make you feel good at any time and it's one of the things that you never get tired of hearing. To me the answer to their question is an easy one though. Although these lessons are meant to be fun and interesting they also aim at intensive speaking practice. Actually, students enjoy them so much they don't realise how much speaking in English they are doing. There is less listening to the teacher, less repeating vocabulary and far more emphasis placed on the student doing the work. In fact the teacher should be giving at least 80% student talk time.

Inevitably in any class, the learner will always show some signs of improvement, but here the student will experience a very fast rate of progression. For me, seeing the quietest of students become the most able and outspoken in class always gives me a great feeling of satisfaction. People leave class knowing that they have just spent two hours speaking fluently with pride and confidence and is why they always return to class completing all 66 topics.

The Keys to Speaking Great English

I was speaking to one of our longest serving IELTS teachers the other day. As per usual we ended up comparing the different styles of lesson and how they related to student ability. Whereas my classes focus on the students talking, the IELTS classes are nearly all centered on the teacher doing the work. Indeed the students just listen, watch Power Point and take notes for two hours on exam preparation. I asked him if his hands were tied when it came to the class interacting and practicing speaking.

"Actually, for the Band 6 and 6.5 classes, if I ask my students to speak in English, most will be unable to talk for longer than a minute. After that they will go quiet just sitting there doing nothing. If we try any form of speaking practice, I have to quickly move on and get back to myself doing the talking. The simple problem lies in that they don't learn how to speak English at school. It's not that they don't practice the basics. They drill lexis over and over and learn grammar in the same way. The trouble is that's as far as it goes. They never learn how to develop an argument or conversation in any shape or form".

It always strikes me as odd when a student's note making ability which may be impeccable, in no way matches their ability to verbalise what they have just written. The education system in the PRC instead focuses on reading and writing facilitated by tests and more tests. A student may have a good command of grammar and an extensive vocabulary especially if they are doing IELTS or TOEFL which demand that what you learn is often well outside of what a native speaker uses in daily life. Most students will have already done extensive ground before coming to a spoken English class.

With all the ground work already done, these classes are very different from those you would normally expect to do in 'traditional' lessons. The teacher's job here is merely to create a pathway to encourage putting what the learner already knows into practice.

For me, after a lifetime of acquiring so much unused knowledge, I can only imagine its like learning to drive for years and years but never buying a car. To most students, the key to speaking fluent English is something that is tantalisingly just out of reach.

Confidence

It can't be restated enough that confidence is the single most important thing that you should be getting from any lesson, anytime, anywhere. Confidence confidence confidence is what it's what it's all about! The most confident and relaxed students will always do better in their IELTS or TOEFL exams. Professional people who are confident and relaxed will always be more successful when they are doing business with Western clients.

From confidence comes fluency and from fluency you will become even more confident. It's a wonderful cycle of growth ending in success. When you are achieving fluency and confidence you will become happy in your studies. Going to class will be no longer a chore you have to do. Instead it will become something you want to do. With no stress and pressure, it will become far easier to identify problems and easier to correct them. You will become more accurate in the way you speak and the puzzle will come together as one whole picture.

There are many ways in which you can focus specifically on confidence building. Here is a checklist of what you could be doing.

- Always remember that you have been learning English for a very long time at school. Remember that you already have a large vocabulary in your memory after years and years of repeating vocabulary, doing homework and tests. I am often envious of my students as my Chinese speaking is nowhere near as good as their English. I have to remind myself that whereas I have only been learning for a few years, my students have been learning since they were young.

- Never worry that your English is not as good as your classmate's and that you may look stupid if you don't answer correctly. It's much better to speak than sit quietly, smiling and saying nothing. Remember that if you aren't speaking you aren't practicing.

- Talk talk talk! Try and speak in English as much as possible. Of course speak in Chinese if you really can't understand something and you want to ask a friend. Just remember that you already have a large English vocabulary so take a moment and try and think of an alternative way of saying what you want.

- Talk talk talk! Try and keep away from using your dictionary as much as possible. Just as before, if you can think of an alternative way of saying something then that's much better than stopping your conversation and spending minutes looking in your dictionary. Learn to talk without pausing as this will make you feel really confident.

- When it is breaktime, continue talking in English so it feels like it is a natural thing to do. Watch lower ability students talk in Chinese during breaktime. Remember you can talk in Chinese all you like when class is finished.

- Always ask questions if you don't know. If you are confused about something don't sit there quietly. There will be other students who are also unclear about the same thing. If you understand what you should be doing then you will feel very confident. If you don't understand what you should be doing this is very bad for your confidence. Make sure you know what you should be doing.

- Get into the habit of speaking in English with the class when the teacher is asking questions. When you answer correctly or contribute to the class in English then it will really boost your confidence.

- Try and answer the teacher's questions before your classmates. Don't sit there quietly and wait for someone else to answer. The more you talk, the more the higher ability students will notice you and want to sit with you to practice their English. Knowing this is great for your confidence.

- Make sure you listen to any advice your teacher gives you. Go home and work on it. These classes emphasise that you only need one or two things to work on at a time, so it shouldn't give you too much pressure and shouldn't be too difficult. If you find that suddenly you are improving because you are listening to your teacher, you will become more confident. If you start to make an improvement your teacher will notice and tell you. This is also a huge confidence builder.

- Help your classmates, especially those who are at a lower ability and may be quieter than you. Help them if they don't understand discussions or activities. Help them with pronunciation, grammar and vocabulary. It will make you feel more confident.

- Learn to communicate with your teacher as much as possible. Sit at the front of the class so that your teacher can listen to you as often as possible. This will make you more confident.

1 Common Student Errors

I frequently get worried looking students coming up to me asking me how they can improve their English before their exam. Many are taking it for the second or third time having not attained the score they need to go overseas. Actually most problems are very common, straightforward and identifiable almost immediately. The real issue is that their errors are habitual, having been ingrained since middle school and thus making them really difficult to iron out.

Recently one of my students was scratching her head wondering what she did wrong in her IELTS; after three attempts the highest she'd got was a 5.5 when she really needed at least a 6. She'd been working really hard and clearly things had gotten the better of her. Blowing he nose into a tissue I asked if she was ok

"I catch cold" was her painful reply!

Here is a list of some of the most common mistakes made in class.
- Basic pronunciation errors.
- Some can be referred as 'Chinglish' which means the direct translation from Chinese into English.
- Some things are straight out of a textbook and may have little to do with the real world.
- General poor use of simple grammar. You don't have to be a grammar wiz when it comes to student correction. After a while you will notice that you are correcting the same errors again and again.

Before you start these classes have a look these different problems that many students have when they are speaking in English and see if you recognise any that you may have yourself. Be honest; you want to improve so really think about which ones belong to you. With a pencil, label those that you think you need to practice. Make sure you work on these when you are in class and at home. Show them to your classmates and ask them to let you know when you are making the mistake. During class your teacher may also refer to this list. When they do make a note at the side of the page and make sure you start to correct your errors. You only need to choose one or two from the list and it's very important that you do this work.

Pronunciation

Refer to Appendix B: Using Phonetics. Phonetics are in British English.

L<u>o</u>ve/Bl<u>oo</u>d/M<u>u</u>d – Phonetics: /lə̯v/blə̯d/mə̯d/
Error: /læv/blæd/mæd/
The /ə/ sound is replaced with a pronounced /æ/ saying 'LAV' or 'BLAD'.

R<u>ou</u>nd/Br<u>ow</u>n/Fr<u>ow</u>n – Phonetics: /ra<u>ʊ</u>nd/ bra<u>ʊ</u>n/fra<u>ʊ</u>n
Error: /r<u>ɑ</u>nd/br<u>ɑ</u>n/fr<u>ɑ</u>n/
The /aʊ/ is replaced by /<u>ɑ</u>/ sounding like 'RAAND' or "BRAAN'.

W<u>i</u>ll/M<u>i</u>ll/Sk<u>i</u>ll – Phonetics: / w ɪ l / m ɪ l / sk ɪ l /
Error: / w i ː l / m i ː l / sk i ː l /
The / ɪ / is replaced by / i ː / changing the meaning of the word to 'WHEAL, MEAL'.

U<u>s</u>ual/Ca<u>s</u>ual/<u>G</u>enre – Phonetics: / ju ː ʒ̯əwəl/ kæʒwəl/ ʒ̯ɑnrə
Many students will be able to make the /ʒ/ sound when you ask them, but in normal conversation they will forget it instantly.
Error: /ju ː ju ː ɔr/ kæ ju ː ɔr/jɑnrə/
The individual may say 'U YOU AL/, CA YOU AL or YANRE'
Many also have difficulty making the last 'L' sound, instead substituting it with an 'AW' sound, for example, 'U YOU AW' and 'CA YOU AW'.

<u>Th</u>is/<u>Th</u>at/O<u>th</u>er – Phonetics: / <u>ð</u>ɪs / <u>ð</u>æt / ə<u>ð</u>ər
Error: /<u>z</u>ɪs / <u>z</u>æt / ə<u>z</u>ər/
The /ð/ is replaced by /z/ creating 'ZIS, ZAT' or 'OZZER'

<u>Th</u>anks/Au<u>th</u>or/Mou<u>th</u> – Phonetics: / θæŋks / ɔ ː θə / maʊθ/
Error: / sæŋks / ɔ ː sə / pɑ ː s /
The /θ/ is replaced by /s/ forming 'SANKS', 'AUSOR' or 'MOUSE'

<u>V</u>iolin/<u>V</u>ery/Ha<u>v</u>e – Phonetics: / <u>v</u>aɪəlɪn / <u>v</u>eri ː / hæ<u>v</u> /

Error: /<u>w</u>aɪəlɪn / <u>w</u>eri ː / hæ<u>w</u> /

The /**v**/ is replaced by /**w**/ forming 'WIOLIN', 'WERY' or 'HOW'

<u>Q</u>uality/<u>Q</u>uantity/<u>Q</u>ualify – Phonetics: /<u>kw</u>ɒləti ː / <u>kw</u>ɒntəti ː / <u>kw</u>ɒləfaɪ

Error: /<u>k</u>ɒləti ː / <u>k</u>ɒntəti ː / <u>k</u>ɒləfaɪ/ Note the /**w**/ is omitted forming 'KAALITY'. Also there is not normally any difficulty with 'qui' words such as 'quick' and 'quiet'.

T<u>r</u>agedy/T<u>r</u>ick/T<u>r</u>ee – Phonetics: / t<u>r</u>ædʒədi / t<u>r</u>ɪk / t<u>r</u>i ː /

Error: / t**w**ædʒədi / t**w**ɪk / t**w**i ː /

The /**r**/ is replaced by /**w**/ thus forming 'TWAGEDY' or 'TWICK'.

Towel/Vehicle/ Critical – Phonetics: / taʊəl / vi ː ɪkəl / krɪtɪkəl /

Error: / taʊ ɔ ː / vi ː ɪkɔ ː /krɪtɪk ɔ ː / Here the learner is unable to make the /**l** / sound ending the word, instead replacing it with / ɔ ː / forming 'TOWAW' or 'VEHICAW'.

Little/Bottle/Title – Phonetics: / lɪtəl / bɒtəl / taɪtəl /

This is an interesting pronunciation error. In the US, if there is a double or single 't' after a vowel it is often changed to a 'd' sound. In both British and American English the /ə/ is omitted with the 't/d' and 'l' being made at the same time, for example.

/ lɪtl / bɒtl / taɪtl /

This allows us to focus on making the 'l' clear and pronounced.

Error: / lɪtɔ ː / bɒt ɔ ː /taɪt ɔ ː /

As above, the /**l**/ is replaced with / ɔ ː / forming 'LITTAW' or 'BOTTAW'. The same applies to words with a 'd' after a vowel such as 'medal' or 'idle'.

The addition of an unnecessary schwa sound / ə /

Orange/Finish/ Few

Error: / ɒrɪndʒ <u>ə</u> / fɪnɪʃ <u>ə</u> / fju ː <u>ə</u> /

This normally happens after the student has said something that sounds like it ends in a consonant forming 'ORANGE ER', 'FINISH ER' or 'FEW ER'.

In addition to this, a schwa may be placed in between two consonants, for example, Adverb/Football/Hardback

Error: / æd ə vɜ ː b / fʊt ə bɔ ː l / hɑ ː d ə bæk /

Sounds like 'ADUVERB', 'FOOTUBALL' or HARDUBACK'.

Chinglish

How do you or can you say (something)?
Error: How to say? / How to spell? This comes from the direct translation of Chinese to English: 'zen me shuo?' / 'zen me pin xie'.
This is the most common mistake made by Chinese students. It is an ingrained habit that you will hear everywhere.

What does it/this mean?
Error: What is meaning? / What's meaning? This comes from the direct translation of 'shenme yisi?' or 'what meaning?'

It's been a while / It's been a long time used if we haven't seen someone
for a while.
Error: Although everyone knows '**Long time no see**' we rarely use it. Chinese students may often use this as it is common to say 'Hao jiu bu jian' which is its direct translation.

I like to use the computer/ play computer games
Error: 'I like to play computer' is less of a problem from direct translation, rather than one of laziness that generalises both statements. Firstly it is missing the preposition 'with' and also the possessive pronoun 'my'. Normally we would say 'use my computer' and 'play (computer) games'.

I really like it
Error: 'I very like it'. This unfortunate sentence comes from the translation of 'feichang xihuan' (very like). Unfortunately the Chinese language has no way of modifying a verb as in English which places 'very much' after the verb. In colloquial English we can say 'really like' instead of 'very' before the verb. 'Very enjoy' is another example of this.

Another problem that can occur alongside the misuse of 'very' is the confusion between 'like' and 'enjoy'. Because of this you may hear '**I am very liking it**'. The word 'like' expresses a state or condition so it is not used as a continuous verb. If used to give approval of something it can be used in the continuous sense though this is rare.

I have a lot of money
Error: 'I have much money'. This common error originates from the use of 'hen duo' which covers, 'much, many' and 'a lot of'. Most students will be aware that 'a lot of' can be used with both countable and uncountable and that 'many' can be used with countable nouns. However though this is possible, it is not common to use either 'many' or 'much' in positive sentences. Normally we use them with 'do not', for example, 'I don't have much money' or 'There isn't much time to eat dinner'.

Text Book English

Nice to meet you.
Error: This should be used only on the first time of meeting. However, it is often mistakenly used instead of 'Nice to see you (again)'.
'Nice to meet you' is also used formally and may be replaced with something more colloquial.

Q: How are you? A: Fine!
Technically there is no error here but in reality native English speakers rarely ask this question. Though this will vary from country to country we would normally say something far more informal. When we give an answer it is also common to say 'thanks' after our answer followed by 'How about you?'

Basic Grammar

Present v past tense
The most common error you will hear is your students keeping everything in the present tense. Though your students will be aware of its importance, unless you remind them they will naturally keep speaking in the present where it is necessary to be speaking in the past or future. Think of as many activities as you can to keep them focused on it.

Why did you buy this?
Error: 'Why you buy this? / Why you like it?' is missing the auxiliary verb 'do', for example, 'Why did you buy this?' or 'Why do you like it?'

He/She
Because 'ta' is used in Chinese for both male and female (him/her and 'ta de' meaning his or hers), they are frequently misused, for example, 'he is going to have a baby soon' or 'she is going to get married to Susan.'
To Western ears it may sound laughable, but it is a big problem for some learners and another difficult habit to iron out.

Give him/her
Error: 'give he/she'. Here the objective 'him/her' is mistakenly replaced by the pronoun 'he/she'. The object 'him/her' is meant to work with a verb, in this case 'give'.

Give them
Error: 'give he or she' / 'give him or her'. In this case 'them' can be used for anyone without reference to sex. Students may be think that 'them' only refers to the plural and so develop this long winded way of saying things, for example, 'When I have a child, I want him or her to be happy' should be 'I want them to be happy'.

Have and Has

Though they are very important when describing possession or when using the perfect tense, 'have' and 'has' are frequently confused. There are only really a few basic rules to this and they are definitely worth remembering.

For Possession
He <u>has</u> a new car/ I <u>have</u> a new car. Error: 'He have a new car'.
'<u>Have</u>': Used with the pronouns 'I' and 'you' and plural nouns.
1: 'I have a class today' or 'You have a student waiting for you'.
2: 'Students have a lot of pressure', 'We have a class' or 'They have a class'
'<u>Has</u>': Used with the third person singular: 'he, she, it'.
'She has a new student to teach', 'It has a written exam'.

'Have got' and 'has got' have the same meaning, for example, 'I have got no class today' means the same as 'I have no class today'. 'He has got a new student to teach' is the same as 'He has a new student to teach'.

Verb Tenses
Present Perfect
'<u>Have</u>': 'I have been to class a few times', 'You have to read that book one day'.
'<u>Has</u>':   'He had to go to class a few times' or 'It has to be sometime in the near future'.
Past Perfect
'<u>Have</u>': I had to go to class before I start the next semester', 'He had already completed the exam before the class ended' or 'They had gone to the UK before passing their test'.

'Have to' as a modal verb: subject + modal verb (have to/has to/had to) + verb
'I/you/students/we/they have to go to class, 'He/she/it has to get there on Friday',
'I/you/we/they/he/she/it had to'

In four day's time / Four days later

Error: 'In four days <u>later</u>' where past and future become confused. Normally someone is trying to refer to something happening n the past. 'In four days (time)' is a prediction normally attached with 'will be going to' whereas 'later' is a simple way to say afterwards.

Let's go and have dinner/ I want to eat seafood tonight

Error: 'Let's go and have <u>a</u> dinner' or 'I want to eat <u>the</u> seafood tonight' It is very common for articles 'a, an' and 'the' to be used with uncountable nouns especially when an adjective is preceding it, for example, 'I have a casual clothes'.

You will also hear 'the England' or 'the France'. Most of the time there is no article before a country name unless the name indicates more than one area is covered or it is a republic, for example, The UK, The USA, The PRC, The USSR, The Czech Republic or The Republic of Ireland. Great Britain is excluded from this list though we can say The British Isles.

This is exciting/ I am excited

Error: 'This is excited / I am exciting'. 'Exciting' is an adjective that describes someone's emotion <u>about</u> something. 'Excited' is an adjective <u>informing</u> you that something has influenced your emotions. Other examples that are commonly used are 'boring/bored', 'surprising/surprised' or 'interesting/interested'.

Further problems occur when a present participle (+ing) or past participle (+ 'ed') are used incorrectly. Always use present participles when the noun you are referring to <u>creates</u> the action. If the noun receives the action, use past participles, for example, "The class is interesting" and 'I was interested'.

One single problem that frequently occurs is between the uncountable noun 'health' and adjective 'healthy'.

Error: 'That is bad for your healthy' or 'He is very health'.

There is not enough time

Error: 'There is <u>no</u> enough time' is another common error. 'No' is never used before 'any, much, many' or 'enough'. It can be used in before other adjectives that accompany a noun, for example, 'no fast cars'.

He doesn't have enough time

Error: 'He don't have enough time' should be 'doesn't'.

'I, you, we' and 'they' go with 'don't'.

'He, she' and 'it' goes with 'doesn't'.

Do you have a hobby?

Error: 'Do you have some hobby?' Mistakes involving plurals and singulars are very common. Here it should be either, 'a hobby' or 'some hobbies'. Often the learner is thinking separately and making an incorrect connection between the adjective and noun rather than seeing them together as a single form. Other common errors are: 'There is some', 'There have some', 'The advantages is', 'The book are' and so on.

I need to go shopping

Error: 'I need to go <u>to</u> shopping'. You can't put a preposition before a gerund. This is a mistake where the learner is trying to do too much and is a sign of uncertainty. Can say 'I need to go to the shops' (prep + definite article + noun)

She works very hard

Error: 'She work very hard'. The simple present tense is one of the most common. Regarding the third person (he, she, it) you must add an 's'. Other errors could be 'He go to work', 'He cook for me' or 'She go by bus'.

I'm making a plan

Error: 'I'm make a plan'. Misuse of the present progressive <u>am</u> + <u>base form</u> + <u>ing</u>
Other examples could be 'She is cook (ing) a meal' or 'I am go (ing) to my office.

10

2 About the Lessons

Here is a list of the main things that you will be doing in class. Sometimes lessons may be slightly different such as the topic 'Giving Directions' which uses maps. Generally though, you will find that things are done the same way every time. This allows you to become comfortable and familiar with this new approach to learning spoken English.

Brainstorm Vocabulary

This is where your teacher will introduce the topic. However, rather than them doing the work, they will first find out how much you already know about it. Actually you will be surprised at the level of your vocabulary. You will probably find that there are some things you know but can't quite recall. When you finally do remember them, they will most likely stay with you forever, especially if you use them in class during your discussions.

Brainstorming means each person in class can say anything that comes into their mind about the topic. It could be a single word or a phrase; it could be something really simple. The first few students to do this will find it easy, but soon some may start finding it harder than they thought. You will start to try and remember vocabulary that you learnt at school but never used.

There is a space at the beginning of each topic to write down any new or useful words that you can use in class. Write these down and if it helps add the meaning in Chinese next to it. Note down any other useful information that goes with it such as pronunciation, placed in context in a sentence or whether it's a noun (countable or uncountable), verb, phrasal verb, adverb or adjective.

Discussion

Find a partner to talk with in most discussions. Sometimes your teacher will put you into threes or small groups. You may have to change partner from time to time.

Selection of discussion questions are based on the following conditions:

- Usefulness for daily life, especially regarding Western culture.
- Usefulness for IELTS and TOEFL practice.
- Keeping a good balance for all students for any ability.
- Making the topic interesting.
- Keeping things fun and enjoyable.
- Special questions for Chinese people.

Going to the shops, asking for directions and answering the phone are examples of the practical nature of the discussions. If you are going abroad or working with native English speakers, knowledge of how we normally do things will move you from academic, text book English to real life.

The 66 topics cover all areas you may be asked in an IELTS or TOEFL exam. Many questions you will find here are also used in these exams giving you a chance to practice and prepare before the test.

Most topics are aimed at everyone within intermediate level. They are simple and straightforward questions that give everyone a chance to create a conversation in English. There is one topic, 'Space and the Planets' which is at upper intermediate level, but other than that everyone should be able to answer and participate in everything if they have patience and confidence in themselves.

You will get to test your general knowledge of each topic and also learn some amazing new things that you had never thought about before. For example, do you know how many moons there are in the solar system? More than ten? More than fifty? More than 100? If you don't know you will have to wait and find out.

There are many activities which are supposed to be as fun as they are interesting. There is a topic called 'Games and Gambling' where some games are played. Apart from that games are replaced by 'Power Activities'. These are meant to be great fun while practicing spoken English especially all the new vocabulary and useful expressions.

After teaching my spoken English classes in China for so many years, these discussions have been carefully chosen to encourage fast learning and fluency. There are many questions that a native English speaker would find strange but work well with Chinese students, for example, 'What is the best age to get married?' To Western people, it's not a very important thing. Chinese students however, will always go into a long discussion about this; the criteria for deciding a marriage partner is a crucial part of Chinese culture. Because it is something so close to heart, students will always try and express themselves. From this comes fluency followed by confidence.

Repeated Questions

Some questions and activities naturally belong in more than one topic, for example buying something can be found in Banks and Money, Shopping, Numbers and Quantities and Clothes. The big advantage of this if you are doing an IELTS or TOEFL exam is that you can make your job of preparation an easier one. If you see something that is in more than one topic then make a note of it.

Past Tense/Future Tense

The single most common error my students make is when they are supposed to be speaking in the past or future tense. Nearly all will speak in the present tense which of course means they are speaking in Chinglish. It is a terrible habit that must be worked on continually until completely corrected.

Most will know which form they should be speaking in but don't do it. If you are not supposed to be using the present tense, a reminder of which one you should be using has been added after each discussion point.

BTQs

Most new students will never have had a conversation in English before, having only learnt to say a few single sentences at school.
'Breakthrough Questions' are aimed at making discussion times much longer and move you up into a new level of English speaking. In this case you will find that BTQ's will have a list of easy to answer questions to accompany them, for example

BTQ: **Describe the last gift you bought for someone** (past tense)
Who was it for? What occasion was it? When did you buy it? Why did you choose it? Where did you buy it from? Describe the last gift you received from someone. Who gave it to you and when? Did you like it? Why did they give it to you?

If you are given a BTQ to answer you should be talking for at least five minutes with your partner. BTQs mean that you are really having a conversation in English. They are excellent for your confidence.

Underlined Words

Some things will be underlined. This is meant to stress an important word that you may not know, for example

Shopping: Think three things you should do when bargaining over something?
What are your special ways to 'knock down' the price?

This means 'reduce the price' but it's common in Western countries to say 'knock down'. If you are not sure of the meaning of an underlined word then make sure you ask your teacher.

Devil's Advocate (Power Activity)

This is a special exercise that will make you speak faster, more fluently and with more confidence. It is an excellent warm-up before the roleplay.

I refer to it as a 'Power Activity' because students become visibly stronger within minutes of starting. Power Activities are also a refreshing change from normal classroom methods while still focusing on the spoken English and the relevant topic.

The one thing I've learnt over the years is how much my students all love a good argument. After a few years, I added The Devil's Advocate so that my classes could focus completely on this.

The Devil's Advocate means that whatever your partner says you will totally disagree with them. You will be given an argument by your teacher that you must use against your classmate. You may not personally agree with what your teacher has given you but you must be clever and make an argument based on what you know rather than what you believe, for example

'I hate football!'(soccer)
If I was given this then my partner's argument would be 'I love football'.
I am from England and I am crazy about football. Even so, I would have to disagree with my friend saying that 'It is boring compared to American games. They only kick a ball around and don't score many goals (points). Football players are paid too much when there are poor people everywhere.'

It's incredible what an argument does to unlock someone's speaking potential. The gains from engaging in argument are:
- Less time in translation between Chinese and English. You will focus on what you want to say rather than how to say it.
- You won't be using your dictionary. This means that interaction becomes faster and fluent. Although dictionaries are very useful, they can also slow down a conversation. In this case, if then you can't remember how to say something then you will have to think of other ways to get around the problem.
- You have to use your listening skills in order to make a swift response.
- You will learn to break free from model text book English.
- You will really enjoy yourself.
- If you are nervous, you won't be after five minutes of doing this activity.
- From fluency comes confidence and a great feeling of self-achievement. You will feel this strongly at the end of the lesson.

Roleplay

Roleplay is where you practice doing something in real life using English such as going to the shops, answering the phone, borrowing something or asking for advice. My students all love roleplay and are happy to do whatever you give them to play in any scenario without inhibition. Most become very focused on what they are doing and really enjoy speaking in English. Roleplay is an excellent way of learning in that:

- Skills that can be used in real life can be practiced.
- You can get valuable look into Western culture.
- You will further the practice of skills and knowledge learnt during class.
- You will feel no pressure especially if you are about to take your IELTS or TOEFL exams.
- It encourages free speaking away from any set models found in text books.
- You will enjoy and have fun with speaking English.
- Great steps can be made regarding fluency and therefore confidence.

Roleplay (Power Activity)

As I said before, I don't often use games in my lessons, though you can find some in T26: Games and Gambling. Instead I often create situations which depart from real life situations. These normally involve argument or disagreement of some kind but are meant to be really good fun.

Many roleplays are set into two parts. The first is normally based on a normal every day activity such as buying or borrowing something. The second involves argument such as returning the bought item as it is faulty and asking for a refund. In this example the customers complain about the terrible food:

Part 1:
Person A: Waiter or waitress. Welcome your customers. Use Sir or Madame and be as polite as possible. Recommend the Chef's Special. Take their order.
Persons B & C: Customers. Order drinks and an entrée.

Part 2:
Persons B, & C: Customers. That food was terrible. Tell the waiter/waitress why. Refuse to pay the bill.
Person A: Waiter or waitress. It's not your fault. Make excuses for the terrible food. They must pay the bill.

Additional Questions and Activities

Your teacher may want to use material from this section. This is in case the class finishes early, you are doing a 1:1 class or they wish to replace a question or activity that has been previously been done in another topic. You may also use these to practice with a friend when you are not in class.

Vocabulary and Useful Expressions

Normally vocabulary is found at the beginning of the topic. However, in this case it is the last thing found after the additional questions. A Chinese translation is given so you can double check your notes and make sure you leave the classroom understanding everything 100%. There may also be something that you missed in class. Do not read this before the class like you would normally do. If you want to improve and also enjoy the class, read these notes after the class has finished.

3 During Class

If you really want to improve there are many things you can do to quickly raise your ability and level of success. Many students think that all they need to do is come to class and do what the teacher says and that is enough. That's ok but there are many things you can be doing yourself which will significantly improve your spoken English without any effort at all. All you have to do is change some of your habits and ways that you normally do things. Remember that when you are learning to speak fluent English you are also changing yourself as a person.

Before Class

• Set your schedule so that you arrive in class at least ten to fifteen minutes before it starts. There are many reasons for this which will be explained below. Don't arrive exactly on time and of course never late.

• Make sure you have worked on any suggestions your teacher made the lesson before. This may be something they pointed out in the 'common student errors' section. You may not be successful in correcting your problems immediately, but the more you work on them the better you will get. Some things you need to be patient with. Remember that if you have done what your teacher has suggested, they will notice during the next class. Teachers love it if a student has seriously listened to them. It demonstrates that they really want to improve.

• Do not read the next topic before the lesson starts, especially the vocabulary at the end of each topic. This may seem very unusual to you as a Chinese person. In my experience, the most difficult people that come to my classes are Chinese teachers who have learnt how to teach in the 'traditional' way. This is normally reviewing and learning all the vocabulary the night before the lesson so that it is easy to place in context and use in basic sentence structures.

However, the Smart English programme is actually just what it says 'Smart English' because most Chinese people already know a huge amount of vocabulary. During class the teacher will be asking many questions about the topic. You will be surprised at how much you already know and how confident that makes you feel, especially if you have not looked at the vocabulary before-hand.

If you answer a question and the teacher says 'well done' then this is a great feeling. You won't get this if you have read the vocabulary before the class; actually you will have the opposite effect.

Eliciting: During class your teacher will elicit as much as possible. Eliciting means that you will be giving the teacher information rather than them doing all the work. There are some great benefits to be made from eliciting if you are a student:

- It is an excellent way for you to use the knowledge that you already have. If you do this it makes you far more confident.
- It makes you much more interested in the topic or discussion point.
- It makes you think about the topic on a deeper level than if the teacher does all the talking.

If there is something you don't know or something you will find useful in the future, make a note of it in the space provided at the beginning of the topic. Writing and analysing new vocabulary in class with your classmates and teacher is a much better way than merely reading the notes at the end of the topic. This way means that information will stay in your brain and is much more effective than reading something.

If you have learnt the vocabulary before the class has started then you will not benefit from this most important aspect of the Smart English programme.

During Class

- Arrive at class ten to fifteen minutes early. This will mean that you will be able to sit with a classmate that you know has the same ability level as you. If you are sat next to someone who is at a higher English speaking level then it may make you less confident, especially if they become frustrated.
- If you are early then you will also be able to sit at the front of the classroom. This is a great benefit if you are interested in improving. It means that you will get to speak with your teacher more often and also they will naturally hear you speaking more than the other students. They will therefore become more familiar with the way you speak and anything you may need to change in order to improve.

By the way, people who sit at the back of the classroom often slip into their bad habits; using their phone or talking too much in Chinese. These are the slow learners.

- Keep off your phone. One of the worst habits my students have is to answer their phone or send messages therefore stopping the activity. If your teacher is explaining something and you are concentrating on your phone, you will not be listening to what you should be doing. In Western countries it is seen as rude if you spend too long on your phone, especially if you leave the room to answer a call. Only do this if it is very important and tell your teacher this before you go.

- Use your dictionary only if you have to. If there is something you don't know then try and think of another way to say it. Remember, you already have a huge vocabulary that you learnt at school so use it. If you still can't think of anything then ask your friend in Chinese to help you. If neither of you can do it only then use your dictionary. You are after all trying to be as fluent as possible. If you are looking at your dictionary then you have stopped talking. The most successful fluent speakers are clever people who can think of alternative ways of saying something.

- Try not speaking Chinese in class. This includes all the small things that we say such as 'thank you, please, correct, sorry/pardon' and 'what does it mean?' Get into the habit of speaking English. The more you do this the better you will get. At breaktime continue speaking in English.

- Make sure you know what these mean before you start these lessons as they are so helpful: *noun, countable and uncountable noun, verb, adverb, phrasal verb and adjective.* You might laugh and say of "of course I know these" but it is surprising how many of my students come to class who don't! Learn these basics and use them often when you are checking on something's meaning.

- Make friends with as many people in class as possible. Get used to changing partners as this will make you become more spontaneous when you are talking. The more friends you have then the more help you will get if you have any problems. Make sure you help others as often as you can.

- When you are talking in English with a classmate, listen to them rather than plan what you are going to say. Listening skills are just as important in any conversation. You need to get into the habit of listening and responding instead of planning. Think about it, do you plan what you are going to say when you are normally speaking in Chinese?

- Listen to your friend and help correct any important errors they make. Some exercises in this book are meant for doing this. Don't worry about upsetting them. You are in class after all and everyone needs to be aware of the things they are not doing correctly otherwise how can you improve?

- Ask questions if you don't understand something. Many students will sit there saying nothing when they don't understand something and then ask their classmate as soon as the activity starts. If are in the habit of doing this then you will start to lose confidence in two ways. Firstly, your classmate will want to start the activity not spend time explaining something again. It's ok to do this for one or two times, but if you continually ask your classmate how to do something they will start to become frustrated. Secondly, it also will promote the feeling that you are not as good as your classmates. This will mean you will be losing confidence.

If you ask your teacher questions because you aren't sure what to do, this will mean that you start the activity with confidence. There will also be people in class who also won't understand and will be relieved that someone has asked.

- When the teacher asks questions, really try and answer them. Don't sit there quietly waiting for the next activity to start. Get into the habit of answering and see how confident you feel.

- Occasionally you will be asked to take turns doing an activity such as in the topic 'Describing Objects'. If so, then volunteer to go first. If you go first then you complete the activity and can then enjoy watching your classmates doing it. This is great for your confidence, especially with no worry or pressure anymore.

- Take notes on new vocabulary or useful expressions. Don't spend too long writing, just the important key points you can use again. You can then quickly refer to them during the activity or after class. Remember that you only get one chance to take notes. You will easily forget them if you don't. I am always surprised when some students don't take notes. People think because it's an English speaking class they need not do this. If you don't then you will miss out on valuable new vocabulary

After Class

- Most students will have only a few really urgent things they need to improve on in their spoken English. Make sure you work on any suggestions your teacher has made. Make this the single most important thing you can do. Your teacher will have identified only one or two things you need to change in order to improve. If you work on this then you can continue to use it in the next class and so on. If you do this, your teacher will notice it and point it out and give you praise. This is a huge confidence builder.

- Do not read the next topic in advance, especially the vocabulary and useful expressions. We have already highlighted why this is so important. Remember you are using the Smart English method not the 'traditional' approach you practiced at school. Trust in the ability that you already have and that you will very soon be speaking fluent spoken English, impressing your colleagues, friends and family.

- Review the most useful and important things from that class as soon as possible. Don't leave doing this until the last minute. Don't make reviewing your notes a chore. Do it as soon as you can and tell yourself that you enjoy doing it. Maybe you can review your notes while you are eating or drinking tea, on the bus or the subway. You only have to read your notes once and hopefully there won't be too many anyway.

4 Topics 1-20

Topic

01 Age

Brainstorm Vocabulary

What do you know?

At the beginning of class, think of any vocabulary that you already know along with your classmates. If there is anything you don't know then <u>write it in the space below</u> and practice using it during class. Make sure you understand if it is a noun, verb, adjective or adverb. Make sure your pronunciation is accurate and that you know how to use it in a sentence. Is it formal or informal?

Write new vocabulary and expressions here:

Discussion

1: Describe your earliest childhood memory (past tense)
What age were you then? What happened?

2: How many kids do you want?
Girls or boys? Why? Who should be the oldest?

3: What age does a boy become a man and a girl become a woman?

4: Did you rebel when you were a teenager?
If not why not? In what ways did you rebel? Who against, your parents or teacher?
In what ways did you rebel? Note: 'rebel' is a <u>heteronym</u> where the spelling stays the same but the meaning changes from verb and noun according to the stressed sound.

5: Open Discussion
What are the legal ages in China for a man and woman to get married?
Why are they different ages? Why can't a man get married earlier? Surely this is unfair?

6: When is the best age to get married and why?
Do you think it is different between a man and a woman? Why?

7: BTQ: What do you want to have achieved by the time you are 40? (future tense)
Talk about career, which country you want to live in, your house, family, lifestyle and any special achievements for example, will have learnt to play an instrument, written a book or travelled to ten countries.

8: Open Discussion
What age do people retire in China?
Is it different for men and women and why? Why can't men retire early?

9: Do you want to live beyond 100 years old? Why or why not?

Devil's Advocate

A parent should not <u>spoil</u> their child.

Role Play

Retirement Home

Person A: You often work away from home. Your parents live in another city. You think your grandparents are too old to be left alone. Strongly encourage them to move to a nice old people's home.

Key words: The old people's home will be *safe, quiet, in the countryside, offer new hobbies, have nurses, soft food and nice music.*

Person B: Grandparent: You don't want to leave. You will feel lonely, miss your friends, routine and your family will forget about you. Refuse to leave. Be <u>stubborn.</u>

Extra Question

If you have a spare few minutes this is a good one to finish with.

What is the best age to be in life and why? I loved being a student as the partying and social life was so fantastic.

Finish Class

Additional Questions and Activities

1: What are the earliest lessons you learnt in life?
How did you learn them and from who?

2: Describe where you grew up as a child?
Which games did you play? Where was your house? In the city, countryside or <u>suburbs</u>?

3: Do parents influence their children too much?
Give examples of where parents make decisions for their children. What would you do if your parents said no to something you wanted?

4: Mid-Life: Present Tense
Person A: Imagine you have reached middle age. Think about yourself at home, at work, doing a hobby. Describe to your friend what you are doing in the present tense, for example, "I am in my office. I have a great view of Shanghai. I am in my new suit" etc. Describe your lifestyle, job, country, city, kids.
Person B: Ask them questions about what they are describing.

.

5: Should people be made to retire?
Should people be allowed to keep working if they wanted to?

6: Is it true to say you are only as old as you feel?
Some people say "age is a state of mind." Do you agree? Why or why not?

7: Would you like to be <u>immortal</u>? Why or why not?

8: Quick fire from the teacher asking individual students
Would you like it if your girlfriend was older than you? Why or why not?
Would you like it if your boyfriend was younger than you? Why or why not?

Devil's Advocate

Parents influence their children too much in China.
They should be allowed to make their own decisions and do what they want to do.

Retirement should be compulsory.

Roleplay

Pocket Money
<u>Person A:</u> Child under 12. All your friends get more pocket money than you. Ask your parents for more money. Don't stop. Be persistent.
<u>Parent B:</u> Parents. No way! You think they already get enough. Give examples of how you already spoil them and why you shouldn't give them any more.

Parents are not happy with their
<u>Person A:</u> Parent. You think your child is watching too much TV and never doing their homework.
<u>Person B:</u> Child. Disagree with your parents. You do enough. You think your parents are being unfair.

You can also substitute this with:
Parents are not happy with son/daughters boyfriend/girlfriend or their choice of degree/major.

Unable to get a job
<u>Person A:</u> You are 45 and have been unemployed for six months. Go to a job interview for an office job. You must get this job.
<u>Person B:</u> Boss. You have lots of younger people who want the job. Why should you give the job to this person?

Fitness Evening for the Over 60's

Person A: You own a gym and will be starting a new class every week for the <u>over 60's</u>. Interview an expert who can teach it.
Continually ask interview questions such as:
What experience do you have? Maybe they were an athlete, in the army, police or sports enthusiast. How long have you been an instructor?
Person B: You are a fitness expert. Talk about your previous experience and your ideas for creating a successful and interesting evening.
Talk about atmosphere, music, different exercises, maybe a theme evening, maybe some special food and drink. How will they benefit from your lessons?

Vocabulary and useful expressions

Pregnant: 怀孕的, labour：分娩, birth：出生, delivery：分娩
Toddler：初学走路的孩子, kid：小孩, boy & girl：男孩&女孩, child：孩子, childish：幼稚的

Teenager：十三岁到十九岁的少年, puberty：青春期, acne：痤疮, rebel：叛逆的
Young man：青年, young adult：年轻的成年人, guy：家伙
In their 20's, 在他们的 20 年代 early：早的，早熟的, mid 20's and late 20's：20 年代的中期和晚期

Mature：成熟的, mid-life：中年, middle age：中年, mid-life crisis：中年危机
Retire：退休, pension：退休金, elder：长辈
Elderly：上了年纪的, old：年老的, OAP：养老金
Death：死亡, bury：埋葬, cremate：火葬, will：遗嘱,
          pass down：遗传, inherit：继承

Topic
02 Personality

Brainstorm Vocabulary

What do you know?

At the beginning of class, think of any vocabulary that you already know along with your classmates. If there is anything you don't know then <u>write it in the space below</u> and practice using it during class. Make sure you understand if it's a noun, verb, adjective or adverb. Make sure your pronunciation is accurate and that you know how to use it in a sentence. Is it formal or informal?

Write new vocabulary and expressions here:

Discussion

1: Describe your parent's positive and negative personality traits.

2: Now describe your own good and bad character traits.
Which come from your mother and which from your father?

3: Do you think you learn your character traits from your parents or they are <u>hereditary</u>?

4: Are you perfect? If there was one thing you would like to change about your character what would it be and why?

5: What are characteristics would your <u>ideal</u> husband or wife have and why?

6: Temper
Generally what kind of person are you? Are you good or bad tempered?

Think of three things that irritate you, for example, someone smoking in the lift or spitting in the restaurant.

How do you calm down when you are angry or irritated?

7: Think of four ways you can use the word 'cool'.

8: Are you a caring person?
Describe the last time you helped someone.
When was it and who was it for?

Do you care about the environment? Describe the last time you did something to help the environment.

9: Good and bad manners
Are you well mannered? Give examples of good and bad behaviour towards other people.
Try and think of examples from both China and Western countries, for example, people talking very loudly on their mobile phones or pushing in front of a queue.

Role Play

Shyness

<u>Person A:</u> You have been invited to a really cool party. Everyone will be there. Ask your friend to join you. No one likes going to a party alone.

<u>Person B:</u> You are really shy. You never go to parties. Think of as many reasons as you can not to go, for example, *"I am too busy, I don't like loud music, I don't like smoking, it will be too late and there may be drugs there"*.

Overbearing Employee

<u>Person A:</u> Boss. You have had complaints that your new employee is irritating in the office. They are too chatty and loud. They don't take the job seriously. Tell them they must change their behaviour immediately.

<u>Person B:</u> Employee. Defend yourself.

Finish Class

Additional Questions and Activities

1: What makes a good boss?
   What makes a bad boss?

2: Job Compatibility
Choose one or two jobs and think of the ideal personality traits for each one.
Would you be suited for these jobs and why?

3: Describe your personality when you were a teenager.
How have you changed? Compare it to how you are now.

4: What makes you different from other people?

5: Think of one thing that people don't know about your personality.

6: Popularity
Think of someone you know who is very popular. What makes them so popular?

7: Is it possible for opposites to attract?

Is it important for husband and wife to have the same personality traits or the same interests? Do you know any couples who are the opposite?

8: Determination (past tense)

Talk about a time where you never gave up and were successful. What obstacles did you have to overcome?

9: Bravery (past tense)

Hero, heroine, heroic, heroism, coward, cowardice, cowardly.

Talk about someone you know, heard about, saw in TV who was very brave. You can think about the Tangshan earthquake where there were many stories of bravery on the TV.

Roleplay

Tight with money

Person A: You are in the restaurant with your friend. It's time to pay the bill. You forgot your wallet. Ask your friend if they can pay for you this time. Be persistent. They have to pay for you.

Person B: Your 'friend' never pays. They said they forgot their wallet last time and borrowed some money from you. They still haven't paid you back yet. Refuse to pay.

Rude

Person A: You are trying to study in the library. That person has been talking loudly on their phone for ten minutes. Ask them politely to be quiet.

Person B: Be as rude as possible. It is none of their business!

Vocabulary and useful expressions

Character：性格, characteristics：特征, character traits：性格特征

Cool：酷的, uncool：不酷的

Good and bad tempered：好与坏脾气的, irritable：急躁的, snappy：爽快的

Short fused：短期的融合

Chilled out：放松的

Chatty：爱说话的

Extrovert：性格外向的人, introvert：格性内向的人

Overbearing：傲慢的

Tight fisted/tight (mean): 吝啬的

Hereditary：遗传的, passed down：遗传下来的

Topic

03 Feelings & Emotions

Brainstorm Vocabulary

What do you know?

At the beginning of class, think of any vocabulary that you already know along with your classmates. If there is anything you don't know then <u>write it in the space below</u> and practice using it during class. Make sure you understand if it's a noun, verb, adjective or adverb. Make sure your pronunciation is accurate and that you know how to use it in a sentence. Is it formal or informal?

Write new vocabulary and expressions here:

Discussion

1: Describe the happiest moment in your life. (past tense)

2: Why are you proud of your country?

3: BTQ: **Excitement** (past and future tenses)
Describe the most exciting time you can remember in your life.
When was it?
Who were you with and what happened?

Describe something exciting you hope to do in the future that will be exciting.

4: Humour (past tense)
Vocabulary: *Hysterical laughter, crying with laughter, laughing until my sides hurt, laughing fit, LOL*

What was the funniest thing that happened to you? Tell a funny story.
What was the funniest thing that you saw on TV?

A challenge: Tell a joke or try and make your friend laugh

5: Depression
Vocabulary: *Prozac, bi-polar*

What is depression?
What causes depression?
What can you do to overcome depression?

6: Fear and phobias
Think of two things that you are afraid of.
Why are you afraid of them?

7: Think of four questions that a psychiatrist may ask their patient.

8: Jealousy, Envy and Admiration
What are the differences between these three words?

Briefly talk about someone who you admire.

9: Talk about something embarrassing that happened to you. (past tense)

Role Play

Visit a Psychiatrist
Use the material from Q7 which should already be on the white board.

Person A: Take one of the flash cards. This is your problem. Visit a psychiatrist to help you.
Person B: You are the psychiatrist. Ask your patient questions about their problem. Find out the cause of the problem and give advice to your patient. You can also try and recommend some medication.

After 10 minutes swap roles so that Person A becomes the psychiatrist and Person B becomes the patient.

Finish Class

Additional Questions and Activities

1: Anxiety (past tense)
Anxious, nervous, worried, panic/anxiety attacks
When do you get nervous? Talk about a time you remember when you got really nervous. When was it and what were you doing? How did you feel at the time?

2: BTQ Stress
What are the most stressful times in life? What are the most stressful jobs and why?
When do you feel stress in daily life?
What are your personal ways to deal with stress?
Thinks of four ways stress affects your body.

3: Love
What is the difference between loving someone and being in love?
What are the symptoms of being in love?
Think of and talk about three things you love, for example, *food, family, best friend, hobby, music.*

4: Sense of Achievement (past tense)
What has been the thing that has brought you the most satisfaction or the greatest feeling of achievement in your life? Why?

Roleplay

Fear of flying
<u>Person A:</u> You are going abroad today with your grandparents. The plane will be <u>taking off</u> shortly.
<u>Person B:</u> Grandparent: You have never flown before and are really afraid to get on the plane. Think of as many reasons not to go as you can.
<u>Person A:</u> Persuade your grandparents to go. Your bags are already on the plane.

Negotiating a pay rise
<u>Person A:</u> Manager. You are irritated and slightly annoyed by this employee.
You don't like this employee. They are often late.
They are often on their mobile phone for personal calls.
They don't complete tasks on time.

You don't like that this employee is the other managers relative. You think they get special treatment and should be treated equally like all the other staff.

<u>Person B:</u> Manager. You are caring and sympathetic to your employee.
This employee is your relative. You know the pressures they have in their life.
However, recently their standards of work have dropped.
They are often late.
They are often on their mobile phone for personal calls.
They don't complete tasks on time.

Think of ways to help your employee.

<u>Person C:</u> Employee. You are depressed and stressed out. Recently you have had some great pressure in your life. Your boss A is giving you too much work.
The company moved to a new office which is far away from your apartment.
However, your husband/wife has said that you need to be earning more money.
You have been at the company for three years. All other staff have had a pay increase except you.

Your Boss B will help you. He is one of your relatives. Negotiate for a pay increase.

Anger: Pizza delivery driver
<u>Person A:</u> You ordered a pizza to be delivered to your apartment over two hours ago. You already phoned the shop, but it has still not arrived. Phone again and ask what has happened. Be angry.
<u>Person B:</u> You work in the restaurant. Answer the phone and make excuses why the pizza has still not been delivered.

Vocabulary and useful expressions

Boring: 令人厌烦的, bored: 无聊的
Exciting and excited: 令人兴奋的与兴奋的
Confusing and confused: 令人困惑的与困惑的
Interesting and interested: 令人感兴趣的与感兴趣的

Interesting and interested – See Appendix C: Common Student Errors
Hysterical laughter, crying with laughter, laughing until my sides hurt, laughing fit, LOL
Turn nouns into adjectives e.g. anxiety/anxious

Negative and forceful: Anger, Annoyance, Contempt, Disgust, Irritation

Negative and not in control: Anxiety, Embarrassment, Fear, Helplessness, Lonely, Powerlessness, Worry

Negative thoughts: Doubt, Envy, Frustration, Guilt, Shame

Negative and passive: Boredom, Despair, Disappointment, Hurt, Sadness

Agitation: Stress, Shock, Tension

Positive and lively: Amusement, Delight, Elation, Excitement, Happiness, Joy, Pleasure

Caring: Affection, Empathy, Friendliness, Love

Positive thoughts: Courage, Hope, Pride, Satisfaction, Trust

Quiet positive: Calm, Content, Relaxed, Relief, Serenity

Reactive: Interest, Politeness, Surprised

Topic
04 Personal Appearance

Brainstorm Vocabulary
What do you know?

At the beginning of class, think of any vocabulary that you already know along with your classmates. If there is anything you don't know then write it in the space below and practice using it during class. Make sure you understand if it is a noun, verb, adjective or adverb. Make sure your pronunciation is accurate and that you know how to use it in a sentence. Is it formal or informal?

Write new vocabulary and expressions here:

Discussion

1: Think of five ways to stay looking young and healthy.

2: Obesity
These days in the West it is very common to see people who are overweight. Why do so many people become too heavy? How have our lifestyles changed in recent years for this to happen? (*comfort eating*) Why do people comfort eat?

3: Anorexia and Bulimia
Many people also under eat. Some people suffer from anorexia or bulimia. Describe both. Why do people suffer from these disorders?

4: What things do you find attractive in the opposite sex?
A turn on, a turn off
This can include someone's personality as well as how someone looks, for example, you might think that someone's smile can be really attractive especially if they have a great sense of humour.

5: Give a compliment
Also 'pay' a compliment. Each student should take turns paying their classmate a compliment.

6: Men and Long Hair
Guys: Would you like to grow your hair long? Why or why not?
Girls: Would you like it if your boyfriend had long hair? Why or why not?

Devil's Advocate

People dress far too casually at work these days with t-shirts, jeans and sports shoes.

Staff should take pride in their company and therefore their appearance.

Role Play

Image consultant

Person A: You are 50 years old. You are still not married and have never had a girlfriend or boyfriend. You have a date this weekend. It's really important.
Go and visit an image consultant and ask for advice on changing your appearance.

Person B: Image consultant: Give advice on how this person can change the way they look. Think about hair style, clothes, shoes, accessories and also maybe there is something with their behaviour that needs changing.

Holiday with the Grandparents

Person A: You will be going on holiday for two weeks with your grandparent next week. Give them advice on improving their appearance. They always wear the same dull brown old clothes. Recommend some bright new, younger looking clothes. Maybe they could change their hair.

Person B: Grandparent. Strongly disagree and be stubborn. You like your clothes; they are familiar and comfortable. Refuse to change the way you look.

Cosmetics
Think of five types of cosmetic product

Cosmetic Sales

Go into groups of 3 or 4. One person should be the salesperson in each group.
Person A: Salesperson: Promote a new beauty product in a supermarket. Try and sell it to some customers. Why will it make them irresistible to the opposite sex? Why is this product so great? How do they use it?

Person B and C: Customers: You are unsure about buying this product.
Continually ask questions about it, for example, Is it tested on animals?
Which ones and how?
How long should I use it for?
What is it made of?

Finish Class

Additional Questions and Activities

1: Describe the most attractive person you ever met.
Why were they so attractive? Remember personality also has a strong influence how someone looks.

2: If you looked like 007 or Angelina Jolie would you like to be a <u>cat-walk</u> model?
Why or why not?

3: Quick fire from the teacher asking individual students
Would you like it if your boyfriend was shorter than you? Why or why not?
Would you mind if your girlfriend was taller than you? Why or why not?
Would you like it if your girlfriend/boyfriend had an <u>athletic</u> build?

4: Tattoos and Piercings
Think of six places on the body that people get pierced.
Would you get a tattoo or piercing? Why or why not? If yes, where would it be?

5: Beards and Moustaches
Guys: Would you like to grow a beard or moustache? Why or why not?
Girls: Would you like it if your boyfriend had a beard or moustache? Why or why not?

6: What is your opinion of high heeled shoes?
How do they affect the legs and feet?
Girls: Do you wear them? Why or why not? How often? How long for? How high?
Guys: Do you prefer a woman to wear high heels? Why or why not?

7: Hair styles
1: Think of six hair colours and six styles.
2: How could your partner improve their hairstyle? Give them some suggestions.

8: Cosmetic Surgery
Vocabulary: *Liposuction, bone shave, facelift, eye, nose and boob job.*
Think of four types of cosmetic surgery. What is your opinion about it?
Look at the pictures. Describe what these famous people have had done. Do you think they look better or worse? Why?

9: Think of four ways you can use the word 'cool'.
Cool can describe someone's appearance, personality, something like a party or concert and is used in place of saying 'ok'. In Chinese people say 'xing xing xing", for example, when they are on the phone. We use 'cool' in the same way.
Use of the word 'uncool', for example, when people wear sunglasses on the subway.

10: Think or five ways to lose weight.
Mention the Atkins diet, liposuction and getting your teeth wired.

Devil's Advocate

Guys: Women spend far too long on their appearance. Women should look natural in order to look good. Girls disagree.
Girls: Men are generally lazy and should spend more time on their appearance. Guys disagree

Roleplay

Weight loss pills
Person A: Salesperson. Your company has some new weight loss pills. They work very well. Sell them to some customers in a supermarket.
When should they be taken? How many? How much weight will they lose?
Person B: Customers. You do think you are overweight. Ask the salesperson about these tablets. Do they have any side effects? How are they tested? Do they really work? How should I take them?

Image consultant alternative
Person A: You are going on a business trip to Shanghai for the weekend. It's really important. Ask a consultant to help you with formal, informal clothing, daytime and evening clothing.
Person B: Image consultant: Give advice on how this person can change the way they look. Think about hair style, clothes, shoes, accessories and also maybe there is something with their behaviour that need changing.

Vocabulary and useful expressions

Figure：轮廓, shape：外形, build：体型, hour-glass figure：玲珑有致的身材
Slim：苗条的, slender：苗条的, skinny：极瘦的, thin：瘦的,
Anorexic：患神经性厌食症的, underweight：重量不足的,
Overweight：超重的 fat：丰满的, obese：肥胖的, comfort eating：安慰性饮食
White lie：无恶意的谎言
Athletic：运动的, toned：某种语气的
Hair: Blonde：金黄色的, brunette：深色的, grey/silver/white/pink rinse：灰色的/银色的/白色的/粉色的染发剂, ginger：姜黄色的, bald：秃头的, wig：假发, toupee：男用假发, dyed：给头发染色, 'comb over'：把稀发拢过头顶
A turn-on：性感的, turn-off：不性感的, 'man-eater'：使男人倾倒的女人,
'lady-killer' 使女人倾倒的男人
Cosmetics：美容品, make-up：化妆品
Cool：酷的, uncool：不酷的

Adverbs of Degree

almost absolutely awfully
badly barely
completely
decidedly deeply
enough enormously
entirely extremely
fairly far fully
greatly
hardly highly hugely
incredibly indeed intensely
just least less little lots
massively most much
nearly
perfectly positively practically pretty purely
quite
rather really
seriously scarcely simply so somewhat strongly
terribly thoroughly too totally
utterly
very virtually well

05 Parts of the Body

Brainstorm Vocabulary

What do you know?

At the beginning of class, think of any vocabulary that you already know along with your classmates. If there is anything you don't know then write it in the space below and practice using it during class. Make sure you understand if it is a noun, verb, adjective or adverb. Make sure your pronunciation is accurate and that you know how to use it in a sentence. Is it formal or informal?

Write new vocabulary and expressions here:

Discussion

1: Are you 100% healthy?
When are you unhealthy in life and how does it affect the different parts of your body?

2: Would you give blood? Why or why not?
  Would you donate organs after you die? Why or why not?

3: The Brain
 Think of three things you know about the brain:
  - The brain is 75% water
  - Bilingual brains. Children who learn two languages before the age of five alter their brain structure forever.
  - When you are asleep, if you are snoring you are not dreaming.

Which is the dominant side of your brain?
The right hand side is considered to be the creative side: dreamers, good at art and sport, like rock music, prefer learning visually with examples, like fiction, enjoy story telling and are cat lovers.
The left hand side is considered to be the logical, thinking side: good at maths, like non-fiction, logical, good memory, prefer structure in their lives, like dogs, well organised.

4: Why do people smoke?
A: Surely it is totally crazy! Do you think smoking is a good or bad thing? How does it affect your health? Would you marry a smoker?

B: What advice could you give someone who wanted to stop smoking?

C: Which of the following would be the best way to reduce smoking? What would the advantages or advantages in each case?

  - Treble the price of cigarettes
  - Make smoking illegal
  - Launch a public health campaign
  - Limit smoking to very specific areas
  - Something else

5: What is your opinion of people who have cosmetic surgery?
Think of five different types of cosmetic surgery, for example, in South Korea it is really popular for people to have their eyes changed.

What is your opinion of famous and rich people who have cosmetic surgery?
Think of someone who has had bad cosmetic surgery.

Look at the photos of famous people who have had cosmetic surgery.
Do they look better or worse after their cosmetic surgery?
Describe the changes that they have had.

Mickey Rourke before:

Mickey Rourke after:

Nicole Kidman before:

Nicole Kidman after:

Meg Ryan before:

Meg Ryan after:

Angelababy before:

Angelababy after:

Sylvester Stallone before:

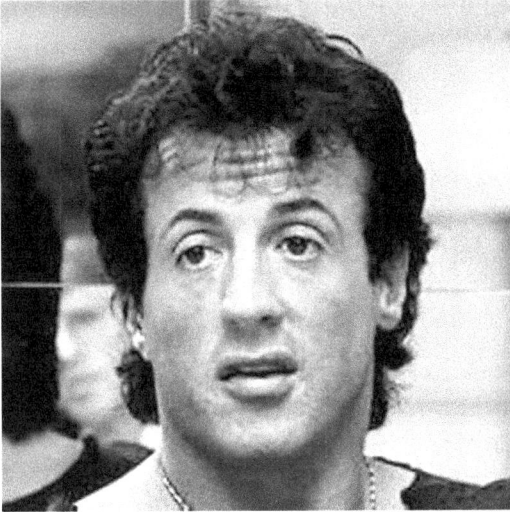

Sylvester Stallone after:

Li Bing Bing: before and after

Devil's Advocate

Alcohol and McDonalds can be advertised.
Cigarette companies should therefore be allowed to advertise as well.

Role Play

Check up at the doctors

Person A: Go for a <u>check up</u> at the doctors. You are a workaholic, working seven days a week under a lot of pressure. You don't eat properly and neglect your family. Recently you have had some bad chest and stomach pains.

Person B: Doctor. This person will have some serious health problems if they are not careful. Recommend immediate changes in lifestyle; exercise, relaxation, better food. What parts of their body are at risk?

Person A: Disagree with the doctor. It is impossible to change.

Fitness Evening for the Over 60's

Person A: You own a gym and will be starting a new class every week for the <u>over 60's</u>. Interview an expert who can teach it.

Continually ask interview questions such as:

What experience do you have? Maybe they were an athlete, in the army, police or sports enthusiast. How long have you been an instructor?

Person B: You are a fitness expert. Talk about your previous experience and your ideas for creating a successful and interesting evening.

Talk about atmosphere, music, different exercises, maybe a theme evening, maybe some special food and drink. How will they benefit from your lessons?

Finish Class

Additional Questions and Activities

1: How does using your computer for too long affect different parts of your body?
How long do you spend on your computer every week/month? If you continue how will your body have changed in ten years time?

2: Teeth
Front, back, upper, lower, incisors, wisdom teeth.
How often do you brush your teeth?
How often do you change your toothbrush?
When was the last time you went to the dentist? What for?
How often you go for a <u>check up</u>?
Do you have perfect teeth?
Would you like to be a dentist? Why or why not?

3: Think of six common places in the body that people have pierced?
Would you like to have a piercing or your partner to have one? Why or why not?

4: Body language
Think of 4 ways we use our eyes to communicate
Think of 4 ways we use our forehead to communicate
Think of 4 ways we use our body to communicate
Think of 8 ways we use our hands to communicate
Which are rude? Which can be important?

Devil's Advocate

It doesn't matter what a person looks like. It is the personality that is the most important when looking for a girlfriend or boyfriend.

Roleplay

Check up at the doctors

Person A: Go for a check up at the doctors. You are a serious couch potato. You don't have a job and haven't worked for a long time. You are unhappy and eat a lot in the afternoons and evenings while watching TV.
You are now overweight and have some serious stomach and heart pains.
Person B: Doctor. This person will have some serious health problems if they are not careful. Recommend immediate changes in lifestyle; exercise, relaxation, better food. What parts of their body are at risk?
Person A: Disagree with the doctor. It is impossible to change.

Cigarette Company

Part 1: (optional)
Person A: Government representative. Announce that from now on cigarette companies will be allowed to advertise in China.
Person B: CCTV interviewer. Continually ask follow up questions? Why is this being allowed? Where will they be allowed to advertise? Won't this affect people's health?

Part 2
Your teacher should put you into groups.
Each group owns a cigarette company. Your group has produced a new brand of cigarette. Think of the target market who will buy the product.
Think of the name of your cigarettes. Write down your ideas.

Part 3
Group A: Your company has a new brand of cigarettes. Give them to people to sample outside a supermarket.
Group B: Customers. You hate cigarettes and what they do to people. You think they are disgusting. Strongly voice your disapproval to these people. Be angry.

Vocabulary and useful expressions

Anatomy：解剖学, organs：器官, muscles：肌肉, bones 骨骼, skeleton：骨架

Tattoo：纹身, piercing：穿孔

Eyes: lids：眼睑, lashes：眼睫毛, brow：眉毛, (wink：递眼色, blink：眨眼睛, stare：凝视, glare：怒视)

Forehead：额, frown：皱眉

Nose: nostrils：鼻孔, bridge：鼻梁

Shoulders：肩, elbow：肘, wrist：手腕, forearm：前臂

Chest：胸腔, waist：腰部

Thigh：大腿, knee：膝盖, ankle：踝

Cosmetic surgery/plastic surgery：整容手术/整形手术, liposuction 脂肪抽吸术,

Face-lift: 作整形手术,

Bone shave (usually on the either side of the jaw): 下颌整形手术,

Nose-job：鼻子整形手术

06 Family

Brainstorm Vocabulary

What do you know?

At the beginning of class, think of any vocabulary that you already know along with your classmates. If there is anything you don't know then <u>write it in the space below</u> and practice using it during class. Make sure you understand if it's a noun, verb, adjective or adverb. Make sure your pronunciation is accurate and that you know how to use it in a sentence. Is it formal or informal?

Write new vocabulary and expressions here:

Discussion

1: Think of and describe four <u>family units</u>.
Make sure the students know what a family unit is and ask them to give you one example before you start.
Answer Check: Make a list on the board that they can use later and explain new concepts.

2: Ancestors (past tense)
Talk about the oldest relative that you know about in your family.
Where did they live? What did they do? Do you know any interesting stories about them?

3: How many children would you like? Boy or girl?

4: Should you <u>spoil</u> your child?
How do you think spoiling your child will affect them in later life?

5: How should you discipline your child?
How were you disciplined as a child? What for? (past tense)

6: Single Parent Family:
What effect does having one parent have on the child? Does it make a difference if it is a single mum or single dad?

7: DINK (double income no kids)
These days this kind of relationship is becoming more common. What are the good and bad points of a DINK relationship and do you think you would prefer to have this kind of lifestyle? Why or why not?

Role Play

Single parent job interview
<u>Person A:</u> You are a single parent. You have a four year old child who you can now send to kindergarten although it is expensive. Go to a job interview for some simple office work. You haven't worked in a long time and really need this job. You have excellent skills and qualifications. You must get this job.

<u>Person B:</u> Employer
You have many other people who are interested in this job. Ask interview questions but make the interview difficult for them, for example *what is their experience? Why do they want the job? When was the last time they worked? Will having a child affect their work? What if the child gets sick?*
If necessary, interview questions can be found in T34: Jobs and in the Office.

Household Chores

'Interrupting': Make sure that you interrupt your classmates when they are speaking in this roleplay.

Person A: Parent. You work late. Often you don't get any time to do the housework. You have two teenage children (B and C) who hardly do any chores to help around the house. They are extremely lazy.
B: Does some housework but not much. They put the dirty plates in the kitchen but never wash up. Sometimes they tidy their dirty clothes up.
C: Does nothing and is really untidy. They leave food and dirty clothes everywhere. They leave the lights on.

Be angry with them and tell them they must start to do the chores.

Person B: You do some housework but not much. Make it sound like you do more.
            Continually interrupt your brother/sister.

Person C: You never do anything. Take credit for what your brother/sister does. Say that you did it.
            Continually interrupt your brother/sister.

Finish Class

Additional Questions and Activities

1: How are you similar to your parents?
Talk about their appearance and their character.

2: Adoption
Does being adopted affect a person in later life?
If a person is adopted do you think they would be like their real parents or foster parents?

3: Do parents influence their children too much?
Should teenagers be allowed to make their own decisions?

4: Would you consider staying single? Why or why not?
In China 'single' means you are not married.

5: Would you like to have an extended family? Why or why not?

6: What <u>makes</u> an excellent family?

7: What <u>makes</u> a good parent?
Would you make a good parent? Why or why not?

Devil's Advocate

The single child policy is an excellent way to manage the population.

You should not spoil your child.

Roleplay

Parent – Your Child
<u>Person A:</u> Parent. You are not happy with your child.
They are watching too much TV, play too many computer games and never doing their homework (or if they are a teenager also you don't like their girlfriend/boyfriend).
<u>Person B:</u> Child. Disagree with your parent.

Going Abroad
You can put your students into pairs or groups of three for this.
<u>Person A:</u> Parent(s). You don't want your son/daughter to go abroad to study. You want them to stay and work in the family business. You hope they will marry a local Chinese person.
<u>Person B:</u> You have other plans. Disagree with your parents.

Retirement Home
<u>Person A:</u> You often work away from home. Your parents live in another city. You think your grandparents are too old to be left alone. Strongly encourage them to move to a nice old people's home.
Key words: *new friends, quiet, soft music, safe, nurses, soft food and new hobbies.*

<u>Person B:</u> Grandparent: You don't want to leave. You will feel lonely, miss your friends, routine and your family will forget about you. Refuse to leave. Be <u>stubborn</u>.

Cleaning Lady
<u>Person A:</u> You want to hire a cleaning lady every month to clean the apartment. Tell your family members.
<u>Person B:</u> Family member. No way! They should save money and do the cleaning themselves. Person A is always too lazy.

Vocabulary and useful expressions

Great great grandmother：高曾祖母（祖母的祖母）

Ancestors：祖先

Mum (UK): 妈妈, mom (US): 妈妈

Dad (UK): 爸爸 pa (US): 爸爸

Niece: 'daughter of a person's brother or sister'：侄女, 外甥女

Cousin: 'the son or daughter of an uncle or aunt'： 堂[表]兄弟姊妹

Nephew: 'a son of one's brother or sister'： 侄子，外甥

Step Son: 'a son of one's husband or wife by a previous marriage'：继子

Ex-wife/husband：前妻/夫

Surname：姓, first name：西方人名的第一个字, middle name：名和姓之间的名字, Mr.：先生, Mrs.：夫人 Ms.：女士, Miss：小姐

Family unit: [医]家系单位

Nuclear family: 'a social unit composed of father, mother, and children'：基本家庭

Single child family, single mum, single dad：独生子女家庭

2.4 child family (Average number of children in a western family)：2.4 个孩子的家庭

DINK: 'double income no kids'：丁克家庭

Extended family：大家庭

Single mother/father, single parent family：单亲家庭

Adopted：被收养的, foster parents： 养父母

Polygamy: 'the practice or condition of having more than one spouse, especially wife, at one time'：多配偶（制），

Monogamy: 'marriage with only one person at a time'. 一夫一妻制

Family roles：家庭角色, house husband：操持家务的丈夫

Topic
07 Friends

Brainstorm Vocabulary

What do you know?

At the beginning of class, think of any vocabulary that you already know along with your classmates. If there is anything you don't know then <u>write it in the space below</u> and practice using it during class. Make sure you understand if it is a noun, verb, adjective or adverb. Make sure your pronunciation is accurate and that you know how to use it in a sentence. Is it formal or informal?

Write new vocabulary and expressions here:

Discussion

1: What qualities should a best friend have?
Talk about your best friend.

Include when and how you met and anything interesting you have done together. (past tense)

What things do you talk about or do with a best friend that you don't do with other friends?

2. How are friends different from family?
What things would you tell your friends and not your family? Why?

3. Tell a story that happened to you with your best friend when you were a child.
They maybe an old classmate or someone you used to play with. (past tense)

4. Do you have any net friends?
How many do you have?
How did you meet them?
Are net friends real friends? <u>How come</u>?

Would you meet them in real life? Why or why not?

5. Have you ever '<u>lost touch</u>' with a friend?
What happened?
Where are they now?
Could you find them?

6: Have you ever '<u>fallen out</u>' with a friend? (past tense)
What happened?
Did you manage to '<u>patch things up</u>'? Are you friends now?

Devil's Advocate

Never go into business with a friend.

Role Play

Make a promise

Person A: You have something important you want to tell your friend. Tell them what it is and make them promise you not to tell anyone. It is your secret.

Person B: Promise not to tell anyone.

Borrow some money from an old friend

Person A: You really need some money. You asked the bank but they said no. However, you heard that recently an old friend won a lot of money on the <u>lottery</u>. Give them a call and ask if you can borrow some. Never give up. You need this money! Make <u>small talk</u> first.

Person B: You haven't heard from this person in five years; no e-mails; no calls or even any text messages. Why should you lend them any money?

.

Finish Class

Additional Questions and Activities

1: They say "Everyone comes into your life for a reason".

Talk about a friend who has taught you something important, or helped you out in some way.

2: Describe someone you know who is popular.

Why do they have so many friends?

What makes a person popular?

3: If your girlfriend/boyfriend's best friend was of the opposite sex, how would you feel?

What would you do, especially if they were spending a lot of time together?

4. Is it important to have friends? Why?

Roleplay

Only an acquaintance

Person A: You are new in town. You don't have any friends and are lonely. However, yesterday you met someone in a coffee shop and got their telephone number. Phone up and ask them to join you for lunch sometime. Be persistent. If they are busy think of another time.

Person B: You don't really know this person and regret giving them your telephone number. Make excuses not to meet them.

Roommates

Person A: You dislike your new roommate and their terrible habits. Politely tell them they have to change.

Person B: Totally disagree with your roommate. You don't like them either.

Go into business with a friend

Person A: You want to turn your hobby into a business. Persuade your friend to join you.

Person B: You don't think it's a good idea. Think of reasons to say no.

Vocabulary and useful expressions

Best friend：至交, close friend：密友
Old friend：故友, life-long friend：终身的朋友
Acquaintance：一般朋友
Colleague：同事
Class mate：（同班）同学
Room mate：室友
Team mate：队员
Net friend：网友, pen pal：笔友
Mate：伙伴, buddy：好友
Friend of a friend：朋友的朋友
Lost touch with：失去与...的联系
Fallen out with：落伍

08 Romance & Dating

Brainstorm Vocabulary

What do you know?

At the beginning of class, think of any vocabulary that you already know along with your classmates. If there is anything you don't know then <u>write it in the space below</u> and practice using it during class. Make sure you understand if it is a noun, verb, adjective or adverb. Make sure your pronunciation is accurate and that you know how to use it in a sentence. Is it formal or informal?

Write new vocabulary and expressions here:

Discussion

1: In China, girlfriend and boyfriend is the usual type of relationship.
Think of five more forms of relationship. There may already be something from the brainstorm up on the white board that you can use as an example.

2: How can you <u>tell</u> if someone is interested in you?

or **How can you get someone interested in you?**

3: Think of five things you should or shouldn't do on a first date?

4: What things do you find attractive in the opposite sex?
You can talk about personality and physical appearance.

5: Would you go on a blind date? Why or why not?
Why do people go on blind dates?

6: BTQ: What is the most important to you in a partner?
Money, Appearance or Love? Why?
Rate each one using percentages, for example, *Love 60%, Appearance 20% and Money 20%.*
You may change the question if you want, for example, by adding personality. This is ok.
It is your discussion to do with it what you want.

7: Would you live with your partner before getting married?
Why or why not?
What are the advantages and disadvantages of living with your partner only after marriage?

8: What are the three most romantic things you could give or do for your partner?

Devil's Advocate

It's ok for couples to kiss and cuddle in public places.

Role Play

Foreign partner

<u>Person A:</u> You are a student studying abroad. You have a foreign partner now and have been living together for six months. Phone your parents and tell them.

<u>Person B:</u> Parents: No way! You don't want a foreign person in your family. You are very traditional.

Finish Class

Additional Questions and Activities

1: Do you believe in love at first sight? Why or why not?

2: What are the <u>symptoms</u> of love?
Use symptoms of a cold as an example.

3: Describe the qualities in your perfect partner.
   Is it possible to find <u>Mr or Mrs Right</u>? Why or why not?

4: Who should pay the bill on a date?
Should men pay for everything? What should the woman pay for?

5: BTQ: **Online Dating**
These days, looking for a partner online has become very popular.
Why do people look for a partner online?
Would you look for your loved one on the internet? Why or why not?
Is it possible to find a genuine partner on the internet? Why or why not?

6: Have you ever had a <u>crush</u> on someone before? (past tense)
Maybe someone you liked but never told them. How did they make you feel?

7: Would you consider having a foreign partner? Why or why not?
Already used in the role play, but becomes more thorough in terms of a discussion.
What are the positives and negative sides to having a foreign partner?

8: Romantic Candlelit Dinner
If you were going to cook a romantic dinner for your partner what would it be? Why would you choose it? What would dessert be?
Or

If you were going to take your partner to a restaurant for a romantic candlelit dinner, where would it be? Why would you choose to go there?

9: Quick fire from the teacher asking individual students
Would you like it if your boyfriend was shorter than you? Why or why not?
Would you mind if your girlfriend was taller than you? Why or why not?
Would you like it if your girlfriend had an athletic build?
Would you like it of your girlfriend was older than you? (toy boy)
              boyfriend was younger than you? Why or why not?

10: If your girlfriend/boyfriend's best friend was of the opposite sex, how would you feel?

11: Should you always be honest to your partner?
Are there any things you would not tell your partner?
Are there any things you would tell your friends but not your partner?

Devil's Advocate

China should have a more modern approach to dating and relationships.
Remind the students to use the examples on the white board, including living together before marriage.

Men should pay for everything on a date!
You really need a class with equal number of male and female students for this.
It's also possible to put one male student against two girls or vice versa if their English is pretty good or they are very outspoken and love arguing. It's a matter of getting to know your students.

Money is the most important thing to consider in any relationship.

It doesn't matter about appearance. It's the personality that is important in a partner.

Students should not be allowed to have girlfriends or boyfriends in middle school or high school.

Roleplay

Can't find a partner
Person A: You have no luck finding a girlfriend or boyfriend. Ask your friend for advice.
Person B: You have lots of experience. Give your friend some tips. Maybe it's their appearance, personality or the way they are going about it.

I have a big crush
Person A: You have a huge crush on someone. You see them every day. They drive you crazy. You can't eat and you can't sleep.
They are very popular and you don't know how you can get their interest.
Ask your friend for advice.
Person B: You have lots of experience. Give your friend some tips on how to be successful.

Parents not happy
In pairs or in a group of three.
Person A& B: Parents are not happy with son/daughters boyfriend/girlfriend.
Person C: Son/Daughter: You love your bf/gf and you don't want to leave them. Argue with your parents.

Vocabulary and useful expressions

Spoken: my 'g/f' or 'b/f'：我的女朋友或者男朋友
Long term relationship：长期的关系
An item：一条, couple：夫妻, my partner：我的同伴
Instant chemistry：即时化学
Mr or Mrs Right：完美伴侣
Compatible (as opposed to 'suitable')：协调的
Short term relationship：短期的关系
One night stand：一夜情, a fling：一时的放纵,
Seeing someone：性伙伴关系（与 Casual relationship 意思相近）
An affair：外遇, lovers：情人, adultery：通奸,
Mistress (there is no male equivalent): 情妇
Two-timing: 对妻子 (丈夫) 不忠
Ex：<口>前妻或前夫，以前的男朋友或女朋友, split/ break up：分手
Single：单身的, available：有用的, bachelor：单身汉, left-over woman (a Chinese term for a single woman over 30): 剩女
'To sleep with' if a student isn't comfortable in using the word 'sex'：与…发生性关系

Celibate：独身主义者

Gay：<美俚> 同性恋者, 尤指男性同性者,

Lesbian and bisexual：女同性恋和双性恋

Open relationship：开放的关系

Toy boy:（指由年长很多的女子供养的情夫）英俊少年，男妓

A turn on：性感的, a turn off：不性感的, fancy someone：喜欢某人,

A crush：（特指女子对男性的）迷恋

Physical contact: hug cuddle and embrace：拥抱, holding hands：手牵手, arm in arm：挽臂，携手, kiss：接吻，吻

Hitting on someone：勾引某人, chatting someone up：与某人搭讪

Topic
09 Marriage & Divorce

Brainstorm Vocabulary

What do you know?

At the beginning of class, think of any vocabulary that you already know along with your classmates. If there is anything you don't know then write it in the space below and practice using it during class. Make sure you understand if it is a noun, verb, adjective or adverb. Make sure your pronunciation is accurate and that you know how to use it in a sentence. Is it formal or informal?

Write new vocabulary and expressions here:

Discussion

1: Describe your ideal husband or wife?
Talk about personality and also if they should adopt traditional roles at home *for example* the wife should do all the cooking and shopping. The husband should be the bread winner.

2: BTQ: Describe the last wedding you went to (past tense)
Who's wedding? When and where was it? Did you enjoy it? Were there many people there? What did the bride wear? Describe the party.

3: When is the best age to get married? Why?

4: Girls: What kind of wedding ring do you want? Describe it?
Material, plain, diamond, gold, platinum, how expensive?
   Guys: What kind of wedding ring would you buy your wife? How much would you pay for it?
Should you both have a wedding ring or just the wife?

5: What kind of wedding party would you like? (future tense)
Would you like it to be in a restaurant or hotel? Maybe something different? Describe music, decoration, food and the speech.

6: Where would you like to go on your honeymoon? Why?
It could be in another country. Which city? What activities would you do there?

7: Parental Influence
Should parents be able to influence who their son or daughter should marries?
Many people leave their partner because their parents say so. Would you do what your parents told you to? What if you really loved your partner or were already married to them?

8: Why do people get divorced?
Surely they love each other and are positive that their partner 'is the one'.
After all, marriage is for life.

Devil's Advocate

Marriage is the end of love

Role Play

Person A: Parent. You think you have found a suitable partner for your son/daughter to start dating with an aim to get marriage. Strongly encourage this relationship.
Person B: Son/daughter. Strongly disagree with your parents. You don't like this person and you have other ideas.

Finish Class

Additional Questions and Activities

1: Why is getting married important?
In the West, many people live together but don't get married. Some even have children.

2: How do you keep the love alive after a long time in a marriage?

3: Would you marry someone who had been divorced? If not, why not?
What if they had been divorced twice?

4: Would you consider staying single? Why or why not?
What are the advantages and disadvantages of staying single?

5: Think of three signs that a marriage is not working?

6: Why is the divorce rate so high these days?

7: Would you 'stand by' your partner no matter even if they make mistakes?
How far would you support your husband or wife? What if they lost their job or were not successful?

8: How does a relationship change when a couple gets married?
This means from girlfriend and boyfriend to husband and wife.

Devil's Advocate

There should be a tough law for people who commit <u>adultery</u>

<u>Roleplay</u>

Plan a <u>stag</u> or <u>hen night</u> for your friend
<u>Person A:</u> You are getting married soon. Ask your best friend to plan a great evening for you. It must be interesting and great fun; a night to remember for the rest of your life.
<u>Person B:</u> Think about location, music, food and drink and something special that will happen during the evening.

Marriage guidance counsellor

Part 1
What problems can a marriage have? Brainstorm with the class.

Part 2
<u>Person A:</u> Marriage guidance counsellor. You are an expert at helping couples with their problems. Give them some advice on saving their marriage.
<u>Persons B and C:</u> You have been together for only one year and already you have difficulties. Blame each other for your problems.

Parents don't like your partner

<u>Person A:</u> Parent. You never liked your son/daughter's partner. They have been married for one year and they aren't making enough money. They have a low position at work. You have decided that they should divorce. Tell your son or daughter.
<u>Person B:</u> Your partner is a really nice person. Disagree with your parents.

Vocabulary and useful expressions

Stag night: 男子婚前聚会（只邀请男性参加）
Hen night: 女子婚前聚会（只邀请女性参加）
Best man: 伴郎, Bridesmaids: 伴娘
Arranged marriage: 包办婚姻
Spouse: 配偶(指夫或妻)
Split up, break up: 分手
Separate: （夫妻）分居, divorce: 离婚, live apart: 分居
Adultery: 通奸, unfaithful: 不忠诚的
An affair: 外遇, lovers: 情人, mistress (there is no male equivalent): 情妇

10 Parties

Brainstorm Vocabulary

What do you know?

At the beginning of class, think of any vocabulary that you already know along with your classmates. If there is anything you don't know then <u>write it in the space below</u> and practice using it during class. Make sure you understand if it is a noun, verb, adjective or adverb. Make sure your pronunciation is accurate and that you know how to use it in a sentence. Is it formal or informal?

Write new vocabulary and expressions here:

Discussion

1: BTQ: Describe the best party you ever went to. (past tense)
When, where, what was the party for? What made it special?
You could also talk about the last party you went to. Was it a good or bad one? Why?

2: What kind of person are you?
Are you sociable and love parties or do you prefer to have a quiet time? <u>How come?</u>

3: Open discussion on drinking
Think of ten types of soft drink.
Think of five alcoholic drinks.

4: Have you ever drunk alcohol before? If not, why not? (past tense)
If you did, did you enjoy it? Where, when, who with and what happened?
Have you been drunk before? Tell your story.

5: What kind of wedding party would you like? (future tense)
Would it be in a restaurant or hotel? Maybe something different? Describe music, decoration, food and the speech.

6: Do you like going to clubs? Why or why not?
What is the difference between a club and a bar?
Describe the last time you went to a club (or bar for anyone that hasn't been to a club before). Did you enjoy it? Describe your night out.

Role Play

Plan an <u>evening out</u> for your boss
<u>Person A:</u> Employee. Your boss has asked you to plan a special evening out for him and some important foreign clients. Tell him your ideas. <u>Impress</u> your boss.
<u>Person B:</u> Boss. You want to impress your clients. Continually make changes to this plan.

Persuade your friend
<u>Person A:</u> You are a student on a Western campus. You have been invited out to a party. You don't want to go alone. Persuade your friend to go with you.
<u>Person B:</u> Friend. You are very shy. Make excuses not to go, for example, *too busy, don't like smoking, drinking, too noisy, dangerous, too late and don't like clubs*

Gate-crasher
Explain what a 'gate-crasher', 'doorman' and 'bouncer' is.
If you can, put your students into small groups.
<u>Person A and B:</u> Gatecrashers. You have no ticket or invitation to get into the party. Try and persuade the doorman to let you in. Be persistent.
<u>Person C:</u> Doorman. Refuse to let anyone in with no initiation or ticket. You are not allowed to accept money.

Finish Class

Additional Questions and Activities

<u>Roleplay</u>

Plan a <u>stag</u> or <u>hen night</u> for your friend
<u>Person A:</u> You are getting married soon. Ask your best friend to plan a great evening for you. It must be interesting and great fun; a night to remember for the rest of your life.
<u>Person B:</u> Think about location, music, food and drink and something special that will happen during the evening.

Drunk Driving
<u>Person A:</u> Police officer. You have caught this person drunk driving. You hate people who do this. Take them down to the police station immediately.
<u>Person B:</u> Drunk driver. Make some big excuses and try and avoid punishment

Noisy Neighbours
<u>Person A:</u> Your neighbours are having a very loud party next door and its 2.00am. Ask them to turn down the music. You have an important day at work tomorrow.
<u>Person B:</u> Neighbour. Make excuses not to turn it down. It will spoil your party.

Parents
<u>Person A and B:</u> Parents. You don't want your teenage son/daughter going to that terrible college party. Say no!
<u>Person C:</u> Son/daughter. You really want to go. Everyone will be going. You must go!

Teacher's handy party tips

These are designed as <u>life savers</u> for anyone who has not been on a typical Western party. Follow these tips for an enjoyable night or ignore them at your peril.

A good night out may start at around 9.00pm at a pub or bar and then on to a club at around midnight. At 2.00am people may go to a house party until 5.00am

1: Always make sure you eat well before you go out. Chinese girls often have a habit of eating hardly anything such as an apple, biscuits or yogurt as their evening meal.

2: Go late. Arrive at 10pm. This has two benefits. Firstly, when you get there, everyone else will be drunk with a long night ahead of them. You will leave the pub/bar feeling really nice after a few drinks and ready to dance. Secondly, when you arrive you will be the most popular person who everyone will want to talk to. Other people in the bar may notice this too.

3: Never mix your drinks. If you are used to it, then this is fine. If you are not used to drinking much, stay with the same drink. If you mix your drinks you may be quickly sick and wanting to go home. Remember the night will be a long one.

4: When you are at the party, if there is punch don't drink it. If someone offers it politely say no. You don't know what is in it. Punch can be dangerous.

5: Never fall asleep at a party. If you are falling asleep and you can't stop yourself go home. For a woman it can be dangerous. For anyone, you can become a target for people's amusement.

Vocabulary and useful expressions

Host：主人

Halloween：万圣节, fancy dress party：化妆舞会

House party：在乡间别墅举行的连续数日的宴会, illegal party：非法舞会,

Warehouse party：大型迷幻狂舞会

House warming：乔迁派对, house leaving party：搬家前的派对

Stag and hen night：婚前单身派对

25th silver, 50th golden, 75th diamond wedding anniversary：银婚、金婚、钻石婚结婚周年纪念日

Party animal：聚会迷, party pooper：<非正>社交聚会上令人扫兴的人，煞风景的人

Gate-crasher：不速之客, bouncer：保镖, doorman：门卫

Club：夜总会, clubbing：参加夜总会活动, going out on the town：去市区玩

Pub：酒馆, bar：酒吧

Stamina：耐力, staying power：忍耐力, lightweight：无足轻重的

Topic

11 Houses & Apartments

Brainstorm Vocabulary

What do you know?

At the beginning of class, think of any vocabulary that you already know along with your classmates. If there is anything you don't know then <u>write it in the space below</u> and practice using it during class. Make sure you understand if it's a noun, verb, adjective or adverb. Make sure your pronunciation is accurate and that you know how to use it in a sentence. Is it formal or informal?

Write new vocabulary and expressions here:

Discussion

1: What are the advantages and disadvantages of renting or buying an apartment?

Note that this is actually four questions in one and they should all be answered thoroughly.

2: BTQ: Describe where you grew up as a child (past tense)
You can also talk about the rooms in your house, bedroom, the view out of your window and the games you played in your childhood.

3: City centre, <u>suburbs</u> or countryside?
Which area would you most like to live in and why?

4: Location
Think of five things that are important when choosing the location of a new property.
.Answers can be positive or negative, for example, convenient/inconvenient to catch the subway, bus, noisy, quiet, dangerous or safe etc.

5: Think of more vocabulary about rooms in a house.
Do this with your teacher.

6: Describe your dream house
Where, which town, which country, what would the view be like from the window, how many rooms. Describe the rooms and what would be in each one?

7: Write down six adjectives to describe a property
Examples are *spacious, cramped, bright and dark.*

8: Sharing accommodation
Have you or do you share your accommodation?
Do you like it?
What are the good and bad points of sharing?

Role Play

Renting Accommodation

<u>Person A:</u> You will start your new job soon and have just arrived in town. You don't have much money. '<u>Phone up</u>' and agent and ask them to help you find suitable accommodation. It can't be too expensive.

Person B: Estate Agent. Try and let your worst accommodation to them. Make it sound much better than it is, for example, *if it's a basement say it is cool in the summer or private. If it's in a noisy area then say it is in a busy or active area.*

Finish Class

Additional Questions and Activities

1: Describe accommodation of the future (future tense)
Talk about how each room would be different. Set a time frame, say in fifty years time.

2: How many different places have you lived? (past tense)
This really means homes, but could be extended to other things like hotels. If you have only lived in one place, listen to your partner and ask them questions, for example, When did you live there, where was it, which part of the country, was it an apartment, how old were you when you lived there, which one did you prefer, when did you move and why?

3: Describe the good and bad things about where you live.
Similar to Question 4 in the main lesson plan 'important things when choosing a location'.

4: Do you prefer older buildings to modern ones? Why?

5: Describe a building that you really like or think is <u>impressive.</u>
Why do you like it?
It could be your hometown, present location or somewhere famous around the world.
You could also talk about a building they dislike.

6: City centre, suburbs or countryside?
What are the advantages and disadvantages of living in each one?

7: House Prices
People say that house prices are too high these days. Why are apartments so expensive? What effect does high house prices have on families? What can be done to solve this problem?

<u>Roleplay</u>

Room mates
Person A: You dislike your new room mate and their terrible habits. Politely tell them they have to change.
Person B: Totally disagree with your room mate. You don't like them either.

Noisy Neighbours

Person A: Your neighbours keep you awake all the time. At 6.30am they have loud children's TV on and until 2.30am they have loud action movies on. You get no sleep and your boss has noticed at work. Complain to the neighbours. Make them turn it down. Be very polite.

Person B: Neighbour. Refuse to turn down your TV.

Parking Space

You will need to explain to your students that in Western countries, people often have their own parking space outside their house. They may not own this space, but it is accepted that this is their area and no one else should park there.

Person A: Your neighbours continually park in your parking space outside your house. It's really inconvenient and annoying. Go to their house and ask them to move their car.

Person B: Neighbour. You have two cars. You have to park it there. Make excuses not to move it.

Cleaning Lady

Person A: You want to hire a cleaning lady every month to clean the apartment. Tell your family members.

Person B: Family member. No way! They should save money and do the cleaning themselves. Person A is always too lazy.

Vocabulary and useful expressions

A property：一处房产

Apartment (US), flat (UK): 公寓

Mortgage：抵押, to let：出租, rent：租借, deposit：押金

Three months rent in advance：三个月预付金, contract：合同

Landlord/lady：房东, estate agent：房地产经纪人, tenant：租客

Furnished：有家具的, semi furnished：有部分家具的, unfurnished：无家具设备的

City centre：城市商业中心区, suburbs：城郊, countryside：乡村

Detached：独立的, semi detached：半独立的, terraced house：英式联排房屋,

Hallway：门厅, landing：楼梯平台

Living room, lounge (British): 客厅，起居室

W.C. the john, wash room, rest room (US), the loo, bathroom (British): 洗手间

Conservatory：温室，暖房

Loft, attic：阁楼

Ground floor, first floor, second floor (UK)：一楼

First floor, second floor (US) The floor at ground level is the first floor：二楼

The downstairs：楼下, the upstairs：楼上, basement：地下室

Adjectives describing property:

Spacious, large, wide
Small, cramped, narrow
Cozy, snug, comfortable, quaint

Light, bright
Dark, dingy, gloomy

**Damp, dank, musty, gloomy
depressing**

**Clean
Untidy, shabby**

Modern, new, luxury,
contemporary
Old, outdated

Beautiful, stunning, fabulous,
charming
Ugly, unsightly, nasty

Describing Objects

Has half an hour of essential basic vocabulary building
that is used through the lesson.

Brainstorm Vocabulary

What do you know?

At the beginning of class, think of any vocabulary that you already know along with your
classmates. If there is anything you don't know then write it in the space below and
practice using it during class. Make sure you understand if it is a noun, verb, adjective or
adverb. Make sure your pronunciation is accurate and that you know how to use it in a
sentence. Is it formal or informal?

Write new vocabulary and expressions here:

2 Dimensional or flat shapes:
Write the noun and adjective under each shape

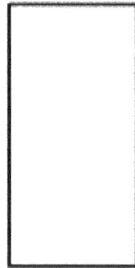

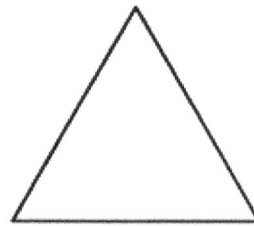

Noun

Noun

Noun

Adjective

Adjective

Adjective:

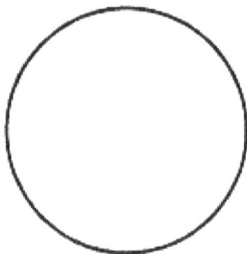

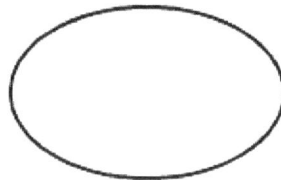

Noun

Noun

Adjective

Adjective

3 Dimensional shapes or volumes:
Write the noun and adjective under each shape

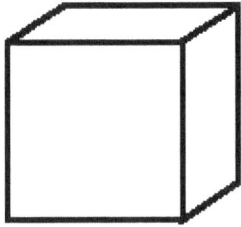

Noun

Adjective

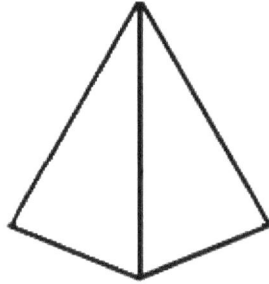

Noun

Adjective

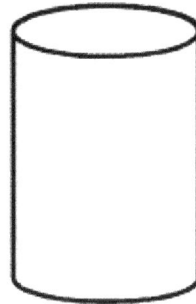

Noun

Adjective

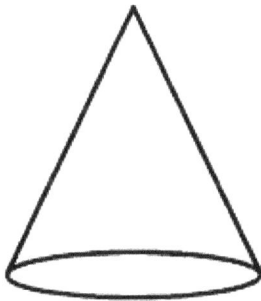

Noun

Adjective

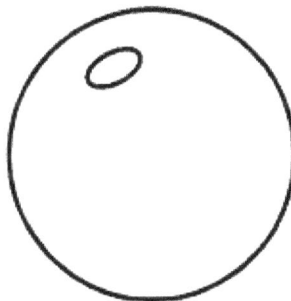

Noun

Adjective

Discussion

1: Guessing Game 1
In pairs, though three people in a small group is still ok.

Person A: Think of one object you would find at home. Don't tell your partner.

Person B: Ask your friend questions about it. Think about the vocabulary on the board, for example, how big is it? What material is it?

Person A: Answer each question simply. **You are not allowed to talk about function.** This includes which room the object is in. If you talk about function in any way, then it is too easy to guess the object.

2: Guessing Game 2
Your teacher will bring some objects to class in a bag.
Take one from the bag without looking inside (you will see the other objects).
Describe the object to the class.
Use the vocabulary on the white board to help you.
You must not talk about function including where it would be found, for example, in the kitchen.

Class: You should listen to what your classmate says and try and guess what the object is.
You can ask questions and ask them to repeat what they have just said.
Take turns picking another object from the bag.
Repeat the exercise as many times as you can.

3: BTQ: **Describe an object of <u>sentimental value</u>.** (past tense)
You should stop using the white board vocabulary.

Think of an object you have that is important to you but may not necessarily be expensive.
Why is it important? Who gave it to you? When? Tell its story.

4: BTQ: **Describe the last gift you gave someone.** (past tense)
Who for? What occasion was it? Why did you choose it? Where did you buy it from?

Describe the last gift you received from someone. Who gave it to you and when? Did you like it? Why did they give it to you?

Role Play

Sell your multi-functional product
Work in small groups of 3 or 4
Your teacher will give you a flash card. Each one has a product on it.

Person A: Your company has made a new product. It has more than one function. Describe what it does to the bosses of a big supermarket and sell them your idea.
Person B and C: Ask questions. Why is this product better than other ones? Why should you buy this product?

Make sure each student gets to try and sell their product.
Give them an example. I always use a white board marker:
"This pen is amazing! It has more than one function. It has twenty colours and will only run out after one year. It is environmentally friendly as you can refill it again. It has a light on it so you can write in the dark and a radio in it so you can play music. It has an Mp3 so you can use it on the bus or train to listen to your favourite sounds. It has a small heater in it so it will keep your hand warm in the winter. Buy two; one for each hand. Amazing!"

Finish Class

Additional Questions and Activities

1: What rooms does a house have upstairs and downstairs?

2: Think of at least five things you may find in each room

3: Think of at least six key words for any <u>household appliance</u>
You may use your dictionary to help you.

Role Play:

Buying a household appliance
Write down six key words for using a washing machine.
Person A: You want to buy a new washing machine. Ask the shop assistant how you use it and other important things you may need to know.
Person B: Shop assistant. Tell the customer about this appliance. Some safety tips would also be useful. Use the key words to help you.

Vocabulary and useful expressions

1: Shape.：形态

Flat：扁平的, 2-dimensional：二维
Circle：圆形物, circular：圆形的
Triangle：三角形, triangular：三角（形）的
Rectangle：矩形, rectangular：矩形的
Square：正方形, squared：正方形的
Ellipse：椭圆形, elliptical：椭圆的

Volumes: 3-dimensional：三维
Go through each noun and then the adjectives
Sphere：球体, spherical：球形的
Cylinder：圆柱体, cylindrical：圆柱的
Pyramid：棱锥体, pyramidal：椎体的
Cone：圆锥体, conical：圆锥形的
Oval：卵形，椭圆形, ovoid：卵形的
Cube：立方体, cubic：立方体的,
A 3-D rectangle is called a cuboid：三维矩形叫做长方体

2: Colour：颜色
Turquoise, lemon yellow, yellow ochre, crimson, burgundy, lime-green are easy colours to remember.

3: Size：尺寸
Forget measurements like cm's; this is spoken English. Instead we use comparisons to other things; we can say 'it's as big as a mobile phone'.

4: Texture：本质
How an object feels. We actually don't use too many words in spoken English to describe texture. These are useful: *Hard, soft, rough smooth* are the ones we use mostly. *Sticky and spongy* are also useful.

5: Material：素材
Again this is really simple. In terms of spoken English we use *glass, wood, paper, metal, cloth, plastic and stone*. This can also be divided up into *man-made and natural materials.*

6: Function：功能
What an object does. It may have more than one function like a mobile phone.

13 Shopping

Brainstorm Vocabulary

What do you know?

At the beginning of class, think of any vocabulary that you already know along with your classmates. If there is anything you don't know then write it in the space below and practice using it during class. Make sure you understand if it is a noun, verb, adjective or adverb. Make sure your pronunciation is accurate and that you know how to use it in a sentence. Is it formal or informal?

Write new vocabulary and expressions here:

Discussion

1: BTQ: How often do you go shopping? (past tense)
Do you like shopping? Why or why not? Describe the last time you went shopping.
Where did you go? When, who with, what did you buy?

2: Where are the best and worst places to go shopping in town and why?

3: Shopaholics
Why do people become addicted to shopping? Are there any times you lose control when
you go shopping? Are there anything's that you just 'had to have'?

4: If you could buy any three luxury items what would they be?
Luxury doesn't necessarily mean they are expensive.
It also means that they are not essential to us.

5: Getting it cheaper
Think of and describe four ways to get your shopping cheaper, for example, <u>buy in bulk</u>.

6: Describe shopping of the future (future tense)
Remember we already have online shopping so you cannot use this as an example.
Be creative.

Devil's Advocate

Online shopping is not as good as 'real shopping'.

Role Play

Buy a briefcase for your boss
<u>Person A:</u> You need to buy a briefcase for your boss's birthday. Everyone in the office
has given you money.
<u>Person B:</u> Shop assistant. You sell luxury briefcases. Sell your most expensive one from
Europe. Why is it so great?

Finish Class

Additional Questions and Activities

1: What advice could you give to a Westerner who has never been shopping in China before? Think of three tips.

2: Think three things you should do when bargaining over something?
What are your special ways to '<u>knock down</u>' the price? In China, walking away like you are not interested any more will always get the price of something immediately reduced.

3: BTQ: Describe the last gift you bought for someone (past tense)
Who for? What occasion was it? When did you buy it? Why did you choose it? Where did you buy it from?

Describe the last gift you received from someone. Who gave it to you and when? Did you like it? Why did they give it to you?

4: Describe the most expensive thing you ever bought? (past tense)
When did you buy it and why? Why didn't you buy a cheaper one?

Devil's Advocate

Online shopping will eventually replace 'real' shopping.

It's great going to the shopping centre at the weekend.

Girls: Men should accompany their girlfriend or wife when they are shopping
Guys: Women spend far too long shopping.
Women should spend more time with their husband or boyfriend and do interesting things together.

Role Play

Shopping Trolley (UK), shopping cart (US)
<u>Person A:</u> You have a lot of shopping. You need to take your shopping trolley outside to the car.
<u>Person B:</u> Security Guard. No one is allowed to take their trolley outside. They have to carry their bags.

Wrong Change
<u>Person A:</u> Customer. You just bought something for 40RMB with a 100RMB note. You only got 10RMB change. They are 50RMB <u>short</u>. Return to the shop and demand your change. This happened to your friend the other day in the same shop.
<u>Person B:</u> Cashier. Absolutely no way! They had already left the shop.

Small Supermarket
Person A: Owner. You have owned a small supermarket for some years. However, a new one has been built nearby. It is very modern. Ask your manager to think of some ideas to attract more customers.
Person B: Manager. Impress your boss with your ideas.

9.9RMB Shop
A 9.9 RMB shop is the cheapest shop there is. In the UK we have the 'one pound shop'.
Person A: Show owner. You have just opened a 9.9RMB shop. Stand outside and make people come in and buy something. Why are your goods worth buying?
Person B: Passer-by. You are not interested in low quality goods.

Vocabulary and useful expressions

Adjectives and nouns of value:
Extortionate：敲诈的，昂贵的, outrageous：粗暴的
A rip off：敲诈, expensive：昂贵的, really expensive：真的很贵,
'An arm and a leg'：巨额花费
Dear：昂贵的, overpriced 价格过高的, steep：极高的, pricey：过分昂贵的
Slightly overpriced：稍高的
Not bad：还好, very reasonable：非常合理的, a bargain：讨价还价, cheap：便宜的
Next to nothing, cut price, dirt cheap
Free：免费的, a give away：赠送

Getting things cheaper：获得更便宜的东西
Buy one get one free：买一赠一
Buying in bulk, wholesale：批发
Half price, fifty percent off：五折
On sale：廉价出售, the January sales（UK）：在英国一月份的大减价销售
End of season shopping：季末降价销售
A bargain, to bargain, haggle：讨价还价

Luxury：奢侈品, luxurious：奢侈的, deluxe：豪华的
Shopaholic：购物狂
Retail therapy：购物疗法
Supermarket：超市, mall, shopping centre, department store：购物商场
Green grocers：绿色食品杂货商, bakers：面包师, butchers：屠夫
Pharmacy, drug store, chemist：药房

Topic

14 Clothes & Fashion

Brainstorm Vocabulary

What do you know?

At the beginning of class, think of any vocabulary that you already know along with your classmates. If there is anything you don't know then <u>write it in the space below</u> and practice using it during class. Make sure you understand if it is a noun, verb, adjective or adverb. Make sure your pronunciation is accurate and that you know how to use it in a sentence. Is it formal or informal?

Write new vocabulary and expressions here:

Discussion

1: Describe your favourite clothes.
Which ones are the most fashionable? Describe them. Are there any clothes you have that you never wear? Why did you buy them?

2: A romantic date
If you were going on a romantic date on a summer's afternoon to the lake or park what would you wear? If you were going on a romantic date to a great restaurant one evening what would you wear?

3: Why do people wear black?
   Why do people wear white and when? Which is most suited to you, black or white?

4: BTQ: When was the last time you bought something new to wear? (past tense)
What did you buy, who did you go with, where did you go and how much was it?

5: Adjectives to describe clothes
Think of three adjectives to describe clothes.

6: If you looked like Angelina Jolie or 007 would you like to be a cat-walk model?
Why or why not?

Devil's Advocate

It is not ok to wear fur

Role Play

Fashion Design
Use the worksheet on fashion design in the vocabulary list below.
Person A: You are a famous fashion designer. Talk about your new seasonal designs for men and women the next summer on CCTV.
Person B: CCTV interviewer. This is very exciting. Continually ask follow up questions.

Buy some shoes

Fill in the worksheet on shoes in the vocabulary list below.

Person A: Customer. You want to buy some shoes. Tell your requirements to the shop assistant and ask for their help.

Person B: Shop assistant. Recommend something to the customer.

Finish Class

Additional Questions and Activities

1: Think of four ways you can use the word 'cool'.

2: Craze

'A popular or widespread fad, fashion that may not last very long.'

Fashion isn't all about clothes. Spend a few minutes giving the class some examples of what a craze is, for example, *Rubix Cubes, the yo-yo, skateboarding, terrible hair styles like 'the mullet'.*

Describe some crazes that you can remember. Where you interested in them and why?

3: Cars

Which car would you most like to have? What <u>statement</u> would it make about you? Again, fashion doesn't have to be about clothes.

Example*: A jeep tells people you are a tough and assertive outdoor person. Maybe you could say practical if you use it out of town.*

4: Describe this year's fashion.

Is it better than last years? Why?

5: High heels

Girls: Do you wear high heels? If not, why not? If yes, when do you where them? Can you wear them all day?

Guys: Do you prefer women in high heels or flat shoes? Do you think women should wear high heels at all?

6: Quality

When you buy clothes how can you tell their quality?

Stitching, double and single stitching, neat and small stitches, shrink, fade, material.

7: Brand names:
Think of five different brand names.
Girls: Do you buy any brand names? Why or why not?
     Do you prefer to buy <u>fake</u> brand names or the real thing? Why?
Guys: Would you buy a fake or real brand name for your girlfriend or wife? Why?

8: Men and Long Hair
Guys: Would you like to grow your hair long? Why or why not?
Girls: Would you like it if your boyfriend had long hair? Why or why not?

9: What kind of person are you?
Do you spend time thinking about what you wear? Do you wear similar clothes every day?
Are you lazy?

Devil's Advocate

People dress far too casually at work these days with t-shirts, jeans and sports shoes.
Staff should take pride in their company and therefore their appearance.

I love fashion magazines.
They are very interesting. We need fashion magazines!

Fashion has gone too far these days.
We must be more conservative about how we dress.

Guys' argument: Women spend far too long on their appearance.
Women should look natural in order to look good.

Guys' argument: Women spend far too long shopping.
Women should spend more time with their husband or boyfriend and do interesting things together.

Girls' argument: Men are generally lazy.
They should spend more time on their appearance.

Girls: Men should accompany their girlfriend or wife when they are shopping.

Role Play:

Changing uniforms
Use the handout on fashion design found below in the vocabulary.
<u>Person A:</u> You are a famous fashion designer. The government has asked you to change the men and women's uniforms for the Beijing subway. Talk about the changes you will make on CCTV.
<u>Person B:</u> CCTV interviewer. This is very exciting. Continually ask follow up questions.

Fashion Design student

Use the vocabulary on fashion design found below.

Person A: Student. Attend an interview for a Master's Degree in Fashion Design. Talk about your work. Why are you such a great designer?

Person B: Professor. Ask interview questions. What interests them about the fashion world? Why will their designs be successful in the future?

Image consultant

Person A: You are 50 years old. You are still not married and have never had a girlfriend or boyfriend. You have a date this weekend. It's really important. Go and visit an image consultant and ask for advice on changing your appearance.

Person B: Image consultant. Give advice on how this person can change the way they look. Think about hair style, clothes, shoes and also maybe there is something with their behaviour that need changing.

Holiday with the Grandparents

Person A: You will be going on holiday for two weeks with your grandparent next week. Give them advice on improving their appearance. They always wear the same dull brown old clothes. Recommend some bright new, younger looking clothes. Maybe they could change their hair.

Person B: Grandparent. Strongly disagree and be stubborn. You like your clothes; they are familiar and comfortable. Refuse to change the way you look.

Vocabulary and useful expressions

Accessory: 配饰

Shirt: 衬衫, blouse: 女式衬衫

Hoody: 连帽针织夹克

Jumper: 针织套衫, polar-neck: 套头圆领部分折反为双层的

Pants (US), trousers (UK): 裤子

Underwear: pants (UK), boxers, knickers: 短裤

Collar: 衣领, cuffs: 袖口

Short and long sleeves: 短或长的袖子

Above the knee: 膝盖上方, knee length: 及膝长度, below the knee: 膝下

Shoes: 鞋子

Heels: 高跟鞋, stiletto: 细高跟鞋, wedges: 坡跟鞋, platforms: 松糕鞋，厚底鞋

Arch: 足弓, sole: 鞋底, toe: （鞋，袜的）足尖部, laces: 鞋带, insole: 鞋垫,
Tongue: 鞋舌

casual   formal   WOMEN'S   MEN'S

Pattern

Seasonal   **material**

Summer   **stripes**   **man made**

Winter   **spots**   **natural**

Spring   **floral**

Autumn   **sports**

elegant   # FASHION

DESIGN   matching

colours pastel light & dark bright

hot   **black & white**

sexy   accessory

Vocabulary for shoes

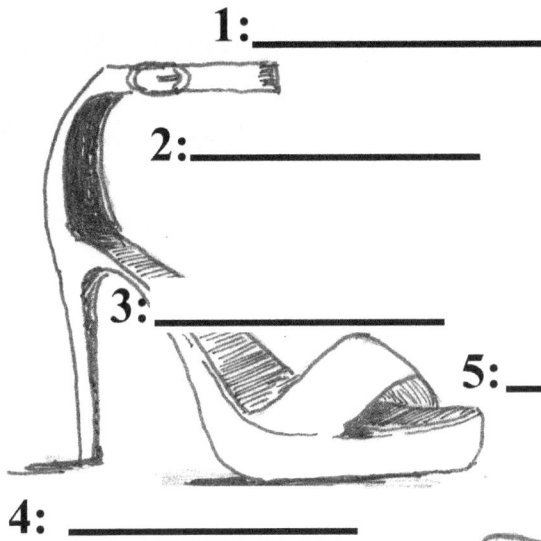

1:_____

2:_____

3:_____

4:_____

5:_____

Match the words to the pictures

heels   toe

laces   strap

tongue   buckle

           open toe

           eyelets

           arch

           sole

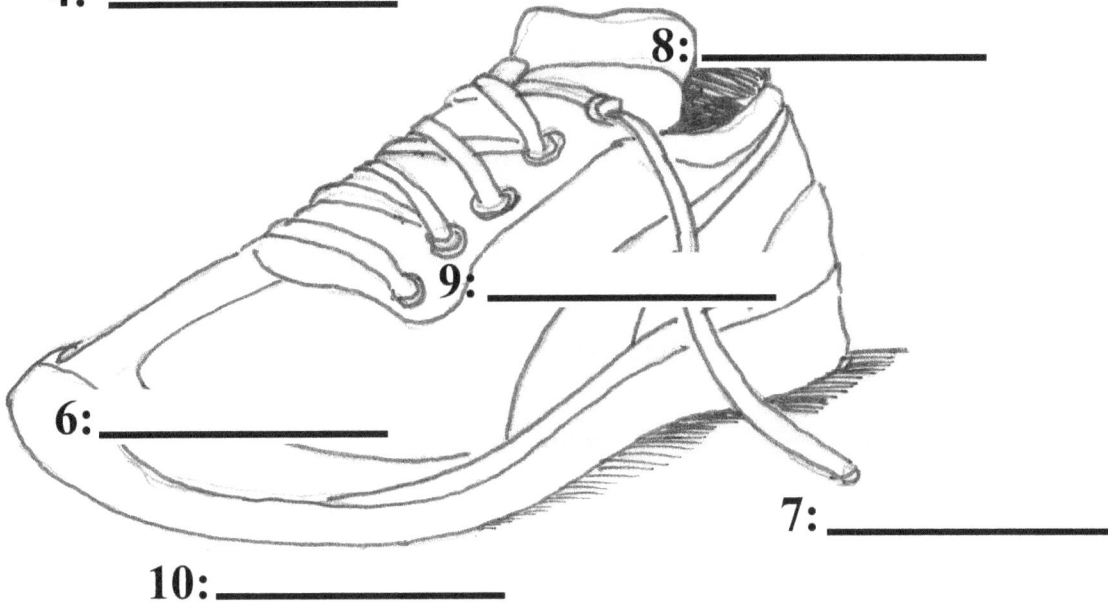

8:_____

9:_____

6:_____

7:_____

10:_____

97

Topic
15 Banks & Money

Brainstorm Vocabulary

What do you know?

At the beginning of class, think of any vocabulary that you already know along with your classmates. If there is anything you don't know then <u>write it in the space below</u> and practice using it during class. Make sure you understand if it's a noun, verb, adjective or adverb. Make sure your pronunciation is accurate and that you know how to use it in a sentence. Is it formal or informal?

Write new vocabulary and expressions here:

98

Discussion

1: Bank Accounts (*teacher's notes*)
Credit card account
Debit card account
Savings account

What is the difference between a credit card and a debit account?
You may not know. Don't worry if you don't. Have a guess and work with your classmates. Your teacher will explain it in two minutes.

2: Do you use a credit card? Why or why not?
If you don't have one would you use one in the future?
What are the advantages and disadvantages of using a credit card?

3: When you were a child how much pocket money did you get?
What did you spend it on? (past tense)

4: Describe the most expensive thing you ever bought? (past tense)
When did you buy it and why?
Why didn't you buy a cheaper one?

5: Found a Wallet
If you found a wallet with 3000 RMB and credit cards what would you do and why?

6: If you won 100 million RMB on the <u>lottery</u> what would you spend it on?
Do you ever play the lottery? Why or why not?
What is your opinion of playing the lottery?

Devil's Advocate

You should never lend anyone your money.

Role Play

Negotiate a <u>pay rise</u> with your boss.
<u>Person A:</u> Everyone in the office has had a pay rise except you. You think you work just as hard as everyone else. Go and ask your boss why?
<u>Person B:</u> Boss. Give an explanation and refuse to give them any more money.

Borrow some money from an old friend
<u>Person A:</u> You really need some money. You asked the bank but they said no. However, you heard that recently an old friend won a lot of money on the '<u>lottery</u>'. Give them a call and ask if you can borrow some. Never give up. You need this money! Make <u>small talk</u> first.
<u>Person B:</u> You haven't heard from this person in five years; no e-mails; no calls or even any text messages. Why should you lend them any money?
.

Finish Class

Additional Questions and Activities

1: Think of three <u>'quick-fix'</u> ways to get money if you had a serious debt to pay off quickly.

2: If you could buy any three luxury items what would they be?
Luxury doesn't necessarily mean they are expensive. It also means that they are not essential to us..

3: Do you overspend or are you <u>frugal</u> with your money?
Do you save money or are you <u>impulsive</u>? Give an example.

4: What is the most important to you in a partner?
Money, Appearance or Love? Why?
Rate each one using percentages, for example, *'Love 60%, Appearance 20% and Money 20%.*
You may change the question if you want, for example, by adding personality. This is ok. It is your discussion to do with as you want.

<u>Devil's Advocate</u>

Gambling should be made legal.

Men should pay for everything on a date!
You really need a class with equal number of male and female students for this.
It's also possible to put one male student against three girls or visa versa if their English is pretty good or they are very outspoken and love arguing. It's a matter of getting to know your students.

Going into business with a friend is a terrible idea.

Roleplay

Pocket Money
Person A: Child under 12. All your friends get more pocket money than you. Ask your parents for more money. Don't stop. Be persistent.
Parent B: Parents. No way! You think they already get enough. Give examples of how you already spoil them and why you shouldn't give them any more.

Wrong Change
Person A: Customer. You just bought something for 40RMB with a 100RMB note. You only got 10RMB change. They are 50RMB short. Return to the shop and demand your change. This happened to your friend the other day.
Person B: Cashier. Absolutely no way! They left the shop.

Go into business with a friend
Person A: You want to turn your hobby into a business. Persuade your friend to join you.
Person B: You don't think it's a good idea. Think of reasons to say no.

Paying the Bill
Person A: You are in a restaurant and it's time to pay for the bill. Unfortunately you forgot your wallet. Ask your friend if they can pay for you.
Person B: Refuse to help. Your friend always forgets their wallet and never pays. They borrowed 100 RMB from you last week and didn't pay you back.

Negotiating for a computer contract
Person A: You are the boss of a new company. You have just opened a new office.
You need a company to help you install 100 new computers.
You want the price to be 500 RMB for each computer installed.
That will be 50,000 RMB in total.
Also you need the job done quickly. Your offices will open in two weeks.
You know many other companies that can do it at a cheaper price.

Person B: Your company will do the job but your boss wants you to do it for 650 RMB for each computer. This will be 65,000 RMB in total.
Although it is more expensive your company is one of the best in town. It is well-known for its professional service.
WHAT EXCELLENT SERVICES DO YOU OFFER?
Impress your boss. YOU MUST GET THIS CONTRACT.

Person C: Your company will do the job but your boss only wants you to do it for 550 RMB for each computer.
This will be 55,000 RMB in total.
You are a new company in town. You can do it cheaper and faster.
You need the money. YOU MUST GET THIS CONTRACT
Your boss will be angry if you fail.

Debt Collection
Person A: You work at the bank. Your customer owes the bank 100,000 RMB. They have not been making their monthly repayments. Phone them up and ask for the money back.
Person B: Make excuses not to repay the money. Try and negotiate for more time.

Vocabulary and useful expressions

Cash：现金, coins：硬币, 'plastic'：信用卡
Currency：货币
ATM: Automated Teller Machine：银行自动取款机
Withdraw, take out：（从银行）取（钱）
Deposit, put in：存款
Transfer：转账
Balance：余额

Credit card account：信用卡账户
Debit card account：借记卡账户
Savings card account：储蓄卡账户
Interest：利息
In the green：账户良好, in the red：负债
Overdraft：透支, limit：限度
Direct debit：直接借记, standing order：委托书
Lottery：彩票
Pay rise, a raise, pay increase：加薪

Credit Cards & Debit Cards – Graph

Many people get very confused about the difference between the two cards. Some think they are the same thing. Some assume an overdraft is with happens with a credit card. The best way to clear up such confusion is to draw these simple graphs on the white board to explain credit cards visually.

Credit Card Account:

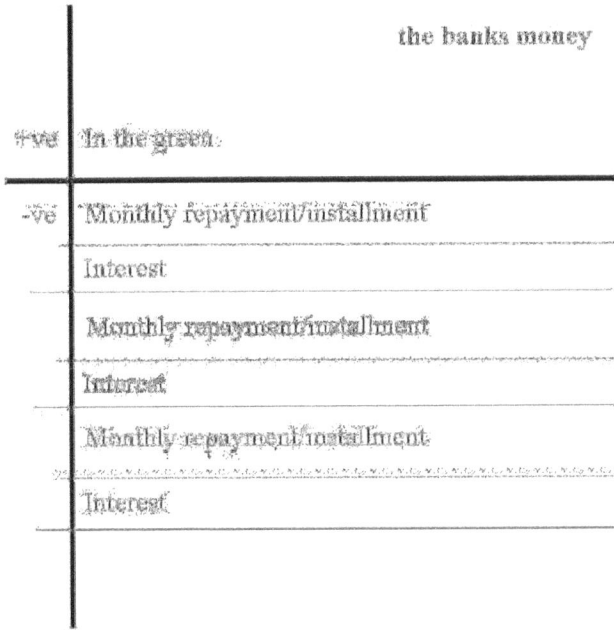

the banks money

+ve | In the green

-ve | Monthly repayment/installment

Interest

Monthly repayment/installment

Interest

Monthly repayment/installment

Interest

Debit Card Account:
(Daily living account)

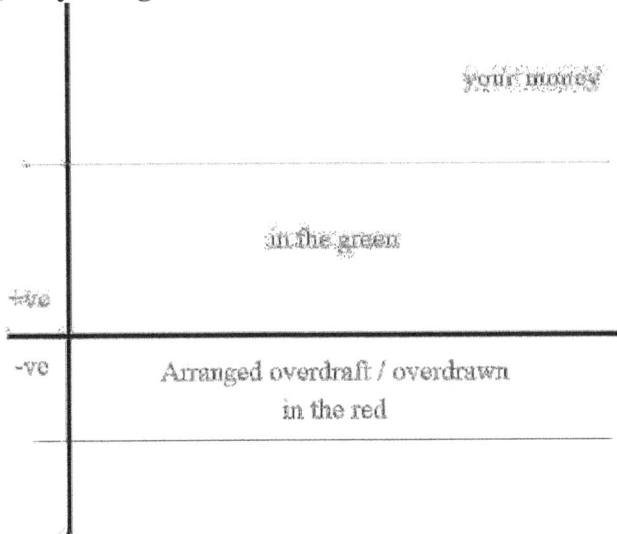

your money

in the green

+ve

-ve | Arranged overdraft / overdrawn
in the red

103

Giving Directions

A fast moving topic where you will practice
speaking simply and quickly.

Brainstorm Vocabulary

What do you know?

At the beginning of class, think of any vocabulary that you already know along with your
classmates. If there is anything you don't know then write it in the space below and practice using
it during class. Make sure you understand if it's a noun, verb, adjective or adverb. Make sure your
pronunciation is accurate and that you know how to use it in a sentence. Is it formal or informal?

Write new vocabulary and expressions here:

Speaking Practice

Exercise 1:
Map 1

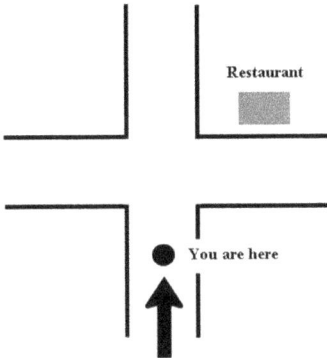

1: Take one minute to think about how to get to the restaurant.
2: Your teacher will ask you to tell them in English how to get there.
3: Listen to how your teacher gives directions and practice again.

'Go down there
tu thu crossroads
turn right
an it's on your left.'

Note: In spoken English 'and' becomes 'an'. Remember that 'to' becomes 'tu' / t ə / and 'the' becomes 'thu' / ð ə /. This allows us to say the sentence much faster.

4: It takes no more than two seconds to say these directions. Say them out loud again quickly and clearly.

Exercise 2:
Map2: The map is now bigger.

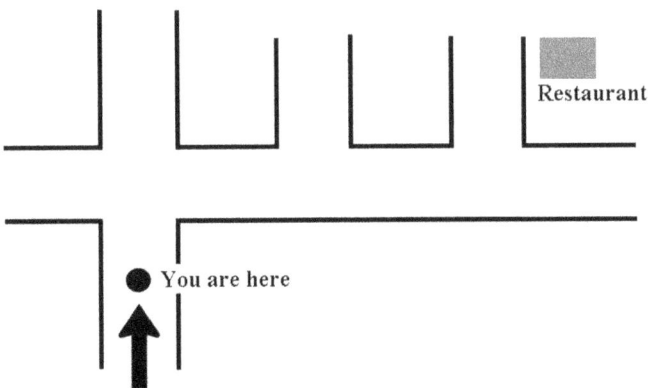

Again, take two minutes to think about this and make sure you practice speaking.

Exercise 3: Map Reading

8 - 1: Go down Oxford Road and turn left at Mill Lane. Go down one block to the crossroads. Go straight over and it's the second building in your right.

___**2:** Go straight down London Road to the second crossroads. Go straight over Woodland Green and it's directly in front of you.

___**3:** Go down London Road to the first crossroads. Turn right down the High Street. Keep going all the way to Paton Street. Turn left at the crossroads and it's on your right.

___**4:** Go down Oxford Street to Paton Street. Go left down one block to the High Street. Turn left at the crossroads and it's the second building on your right.

___**5:** Go down London Road to the High Street. Turn right and go down two blocks to the crossroads at Paton Street and it's on the first corner on your left.

___**6:** Go down London Road two blocks to Woodland Green and turn right. Go down another two blocks to the crossroads before Cedar Close then turn right. Go straight over the first crossroads on Paton Street and it's on your left.

___**7:** Go straight down Oxford Road to the crossroads on Mill Lane. Turn left until you get to High Street. Go straight over and it's on your left.

___**8:** Go down London Road to High Street. When you get there take a right. When you reach Mill Lane you will see it opposite you on the left hand corner of the crossroads.

___**9:** Go all the way down Oxford Road two blocks until you reach Paton Street. Turn left and then left again down High Street. At the first crossroads go right to Woodland Green. When you get there you will see it opposite you on the right.

___**10:** Go straight down London Road to Woodland Green. Turn right and go down two blocks until you reach Cedar Close. It's on your left down Cedar Close.

Exercise 4: Worksheet

There are two maps: Map A and Map B. You will notice that they are of the same area but they have different places marked on each one.

Work with a classmate in pairs. One person should have Map A and the other should have Map B. Make sure that your partner does not look at your map.
Starting at the same place marked 'You are here', you should then take turns asking for directions for the places written at the top. These will be marked on your classmates map but not yours, for example,
Map A student *"Excuse me. Could you tell me the way to the police station please?"*
This will be marked on your partner's map. Your classmate should then give you directions. Follow the instructions and try and find the right place.

Map A: Ask your classmate for directions.

"Excuse me. Could you tell me the way to the _____ please?

These places are not on your map. They are on Map B

1: School   2: Department store   3: The train station

4: Bakery   5: The wine bar   6: Police station

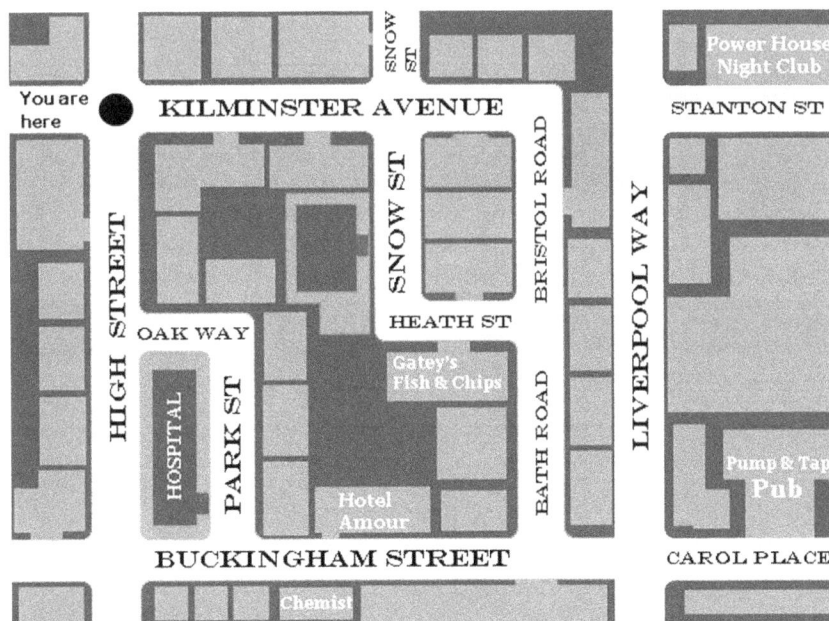

Map B: Ask your classmate for directions.

"Excuse me. Could you tell me the way to the _____ please?

These places are not on your map. They are on Map A

1: Hospital   **2: Night Club**   **3: Fish & chip shop**

4: Hotel   **5: Chemist**   **6: Pub**

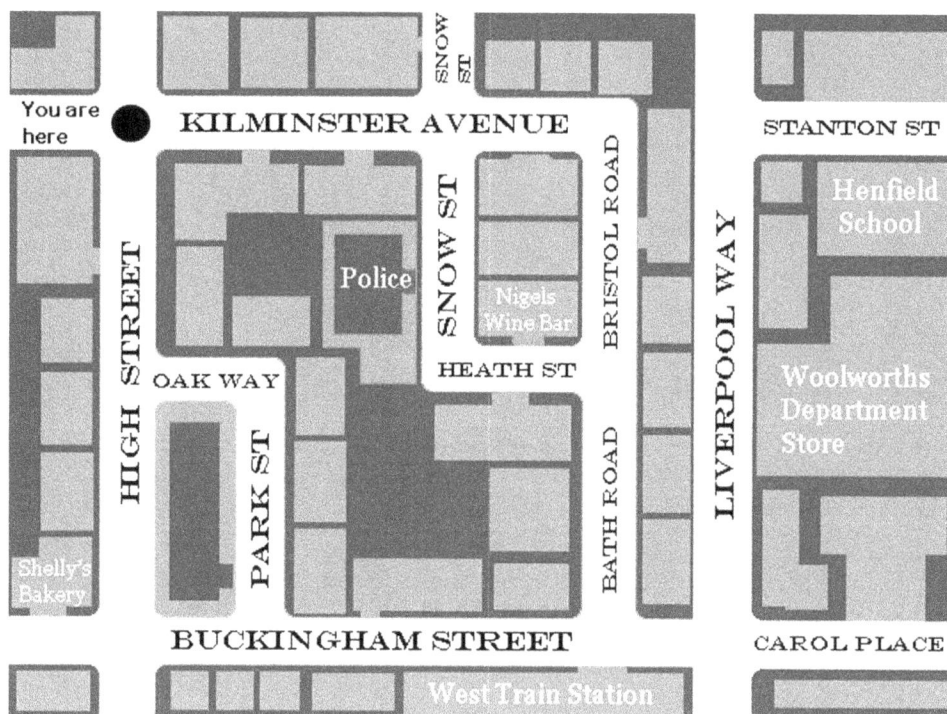

Role Play

Roleplay Asking for directions on the phone

The locations from Exercise 4 are now put together making one map with some additions.
The starting point has been changed. The students need to find the GLC Offices on the
left hand side of the map.

Person A:

You have an important job interview today at the GLC Offices.

Your taxi driver has dropped you at the wrong place **"You are here"**.

Phone the office and ask for directions. You are lost and very confused.
Continually ask the receptionist questions. Make it difficult for them.

Person B:

Receptionist. Politely give them directions.

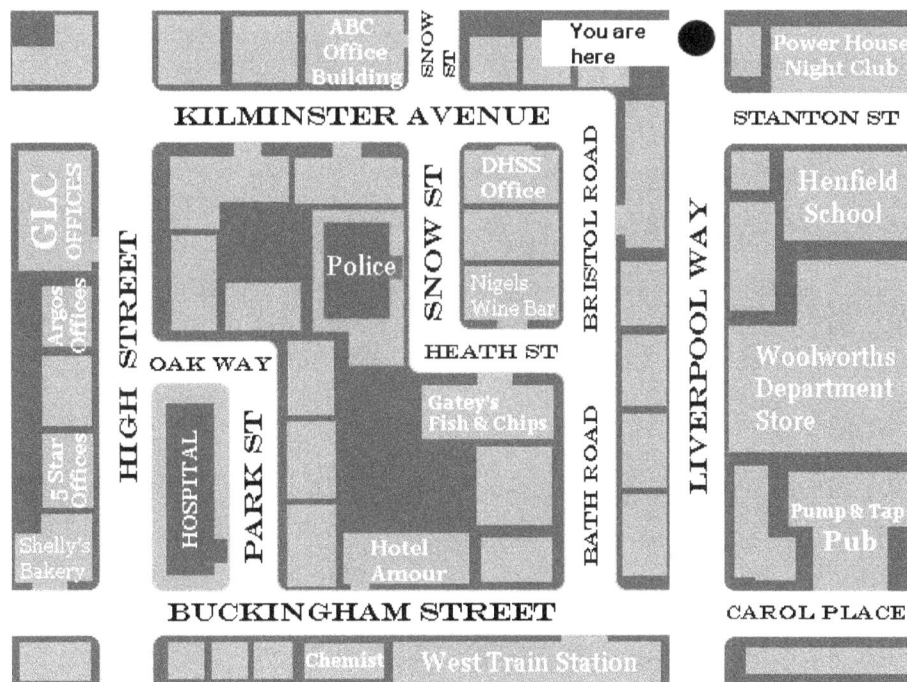

Speaking Practice

Exercise 5: Map3: The map is now bigger.

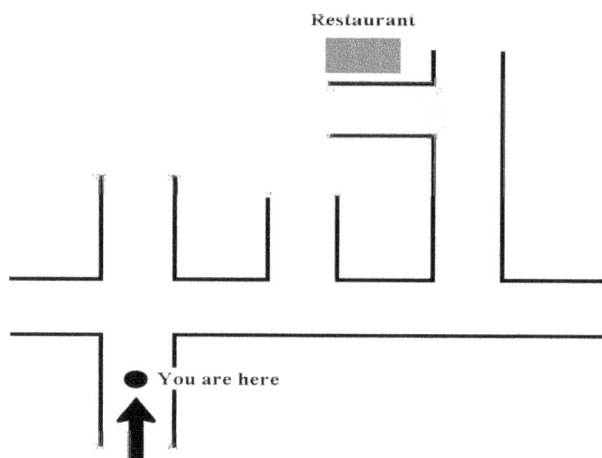

1: Take one minute to think about how to get to the restaurant.
2: Your teacher will ask you to tell them in English how to get there.
3: Listen to how your teacher gives directions and practice again.
4: It takes no more than two seconds to say these directions. Say them out loud again quickly and clearly. Try to be as fluent as possible.

Finish Class

Vocabulary and useful expressions

Right：右边的, left：左边的, go straight ahead/on：直走
Straight over：直走, straight across：穿过
Landmarks：陆标
Junction/intersection：十字路口, crossroads：十字路口
Roundabout (UK), traffic circle (US): 环形交通枢纽
Clockwise：顺时针方向的, anti-clockwise：逆时针方向的, first exit：第一个出口
T-junction：丁字路口
Traffic lights, red, amber, green：交通灯（红、黄、绿）
Zebra crossing, cross walk (some parts of US): 斑马线，人行横道
Over/under pass：天桥/地下通道
Pedestrian：行人, pavement (UK), sidewalk (US): 人行道

Topic
17 Numbers & Quantities

Brainstorm Vocabulary

What do you know?

At the beginning of class, think of any vocabulary that you already know along with your classmates. If there is anything you don't know then write it in the space below and practice using it during class. Make sure you understand if it is a noun, verb, adjective or adverb. Make sure your pronunciation is accurate and that you know how to use it in a sentence. Is it formal or informal?

Write new vocabulary and expressions here:

111

Discussion

1: Basic maths (past tense)
Did you enjoy maths when you were at school? Why or why not?
What part of it did you enjoy or hate the most?
There may be some vocabulary that you don't know so make sure you ask your teacher to explain it for you.

2: Basic maths exercises
Work in pairs.
Use one of the two question sheets each. Make sure your classmate does not see yours.
Ask each other the questions in spoken English.
When your classmate answers they should give the whole answer, for example, "five plus five is/equals ten" not simply "ten".

Basic Maths A:

Spoken English Vocabulary:
+ plus (and), - minus, x times, / divided by, = is/equals, 0.5 naught point five
½ a half, 1/3 a third, ¼ a quarter, 1/5 a fifth

What's five plus five? Ten or you can say **Five plus five is ten/ equals ten**

Questions: Ask these questions to your friend. They can use a <u>calculator</u> to help

1: $6 + 6 =$?   **2:** $100 - 33 =$?   **3:** $99 / 3 =$?   **4:** $668 \times 8 =$? **5:** $10 - 6868 =$?

6: What is their telephone number? They should answer you as fast as possible. They should tell you two times.

Basic Maths B:

Spoken English Vocabulary:
+ plus (and), - minus, x times, / divided by, = is/equals, 0.5 naught point five
½ a half, 1/3 a third, ¼ a quarter, 1/5 a fifth

What's five plus five? Ten or you can say **Five plus five is ten/ equals ten**

Questions: Ask these questions to your friend. They can use a <u>calculator</u> to help

1: 338 + 338 =? **2:** 886 – 668 =? **3:** 6 / 8 =? **4:** 77 x 33 =? **5:** 10 – 70.6868 =?

6: What is their telephone number? They should answer you as fast as possible. They should tell you two times.

3: BTQ: **Distance**
Describe your longest journey. How long was it in time and distance? Who with, when, why did you go on the journey, what transport did you use, did you have to transfer? If you had to transfer, how long was each stage of the journey? (past tense)

4: Time
Before the discussion in Q5, look at this basic spoken vocabulary:

Q: Think of two ways to say 6.30
   Think of two ways to say 6.15
   Think of two ways to say 6.23
   Think of three ways to say 6.56
   Think of another way to say 6.03

5: Time: Your daily schedule
Work in pairs. Tell your classmate about your daily schedule. When do you normally get up, have breakfast, go out, work or college routine, lunch, evening meal, go home, relax/personal interests and go to bed.
This is an important listening exercise so pay attention to what your classmate says and not what you are going to say.

6: Lucky numbers
What are the lucky and unlucky numbers in China and what do they mean? Do you have any of these numbers on your phone? Answer Check

Devil's Advocate

After school is finished we normally forget most of the maths we learnt. Maths should therefore not be a <u>compulsory</u> subject.

Role Play

Only an acquaintance

<u>Person A:</u> You are new in town. You don't have any friends and are lonely. However, yesterday you met someone in a coffee shop and got their telephone number. <u>Phone them up</u> and ask them to join you for lunch sometime. Be persistent. If they are busy think of another time.
<u>Person B:</u> You don't really know this person and <u>regret</u> giving them your telephone number. Make excuses not to meet them.

You are late
<u>Person A:</u> You have been waiting for your friend for half an hour. Phone them and ask them where they are. They are always late! Mention the time they should have arrived and the reason for you meeting up.
<u>Person B:</u> Make an excuse. You will be there shortly.

Finish Class

Additional Questions and Activities

1: Time. Are you a good time keeper or are you sometimes late?
How often?

2: Time. Describe the last time you were late. (past tense) Why were you late?

3: Time. If you were a manager, what would you do if an employee was late?
How about for a second and third time?

4: Temperature
Think of three verbs we can use when water changes temperature, for example, 'freeze'. Try and think of the nouns that go with them, for example, 'ice'.

5: Temperature (past tense)
2008 'China's Year'. Talk about what happened across China during January and February of 2008.

6: Speed
What is the fastest vehicle ever made?
What is the fastest animal? How fast can it go? How is it able to go so fast?

7: Lottery
Do you play the lottery? Why or why not? What is your opinion of people who play the lottery?

Roleplay

Bad Driving
Person A: Traffic Police. You have caught that person driving too fast across a red light. Your computer says this is the second time they have done this. You don't like drivers who drive too fast. Give them a heavy fine.
Person B: Driver. Make an excuse. Avoid paying the fine.

Negotiating for a computer contract
Person A: You are the boss of a new company. You have just opened a new office.
You need a company to help you <u>install</u> 100 new computers.
You want the price to be 500 RMB for each computer installed.
That will be 50,000 RMB in total.
Also you need the job done quickly. Your offices will open in two weeks.
You know many other companies that can do it at a cheaper price.

Person B: Your company will do the job but your boss wants you to do it for 650 RMB for each computer. This will be 65,000 RMB in total.
Although it is more expensive your company is one of the best in town. It is well-known for its professional service.
WHAT EXCELLENT SERVICES DO YOU OFFER?
Impress your boss. YOU MUST GET THIS CONTRACT.

Person C: Your company will do the job but your boss only wants you to do it for 550 RMB for each computer.
This will be 55,000 RMB in total.
You are a new company in town. You can do it cheaper and faster.
You need the money. YOU MUST GET THIS CONTRACT
Your boss will be angry if you fail.

Vocabulary and useful expressions

Math (US), Maths (UK). : 数学

On the dot：准时地, bang on 10：10 点整

Around 10, 10ish：差不多 10 点

Coming up to seven, almost seven : 就快到七点的

Just past six : 刚刚过六点

Round off the number：舍入整数

 a round number：平头数（〈方〉：十、百、千、万等不带零头的整数）

Imperial : 度量衡英制的, metric : 公制的

Topic

18 Food

Brainstorm Vocabulary

What do you know?

At the beginning of class, think of any vocabulary that you already know along with your classmates. If there is anything you don't know then <u>write it in the space below</u> and practice using it during class. Make sure you understand if it is a noun, verb, adjective or adverb. Make sure your pronunciation is accurate and that you know how to use it in a sentence. Is it formal or informal?

Write new vocabulary and expressions here:

117

Discussion

1: Do you have a healthy balanced diet?
Do you have a perfect diet? What is missing from your diet?
Do you eat any unhealthy food? Why is it unhealthy and what does it do to your body?

2: Food Safety
Food safety is a huge issue now in China. Give examples of food which may be dangerous to eat. Why does China have this problem?

3: Which is the unhealthiest food? Why?

4: McDonald's and KFC
Do you eat at McDonald's or KFC? How often? Think of five positive and five negative points about eating in these places.

5: What is a vegetarian? What can a vegetarian eat?
Ask the class and do this quickly, making a list on the white board for the Devil's Advocate later.
What is a vegan? If you only eat fish but not meat are you still a vegetarian?
"I'm a vegetarian but sometimes I eat some chicken." What is your opinion about this statement?

6: Think of five ways to lose weight.

7: What did you have to eat yesterday? (past tense)
In pairs tell your classmate what you had for breakfast, lunch and dinner yesterday.
Did you enjoy it? What food do you love and hate?
Take turns doing this. One of you should do the talking and the other should listen. Change after 2 minutes.

Devil's Advocate

I want to be a vegetarian and I want you to join me.

Role Play

Over 60's Evening

Person A: You own a restaurant. You want to start an <u>over 60's</u> evening for the older people in your neighbourhood. Hire an expert chef to manage the evening.
Ask interview questions such as "What is your experience? Why are you interested in the job? How long have you been a chef?"
Person B: Expert Chef. Answer all questions. What special ideas do you have for over 60's evening?

Finish Class

Additional Questions and Activities

These can be also be used in T19: Cooking and T20: Eating out

1: GM Food
What is GM food?
What are the advantages and disadvantages of GM food?

2: British English v American English
Think of three differences between British and American food vocabulary.

3: Would you eat dog? Why or why not?
How about cat?

4: Is there any really expensive food you like?
What is it and how often do you have it?
When was the last time you had it?
Where did you have it?
Who was it with and what occasion was it? (past tense)

5: BTQ: **What was the most expensive restaurant you ever went to?** (past tense)
Where was it? When did you go? Who with?
What did you have? How was the food?
Why did you go there? Was it a special occasion?

6: BTQ: **What is the best food in China?**
Why? Where is it from? How is it made? What's the worst? Why and where is it from?

7: BTQ: **Have you ever been to a restaurant when the food was bad?**
Where was it? Why was it so terrible? When did you go? Who with? How was the service? (past tense)

8: Steak
How often do you eat steak? How do you like it cooked? (We often use the word 'done' instead of cooked)

Devil's Advocate

All men should be able to cook for their girlfriend or wife

A vegetarian should not be able to eat fish

McDonalds is great place. Mmmm, it's delicious, healthy and nutritious.

Role Play:

Hire a new waiter/waitress
Person A: You own a restaurant (choose cuisine). Hire a new waitress/waiter.
Ask interview questions.
Why did you want to work in a restaurant? How do you take an order? What do you do if something is wrong?
Person B: Answer all the questions. Get the job!

Gluttonous member of staff
Person A: Boss. Your new member of staff is always eating in the office. Tell them that it must stop. You have already told them once before.
Person B: Employee. You work so hard you have to eat in the office.

Best Pizza
Person A: Congratulations. Your shop has won an award for the best pizza in town.
Talk about what different flavours you have on your menu.
Person B: CCTV interviewer. Continually ask follow up questions.

Pizza delivery driver
Person A: You ordered a pizza to be delivered to your apartment over two hours ago.
You already phoned the shop, but it has still not arrived. Phone again and ask what has happened. Be angry.
Person B: You work in the restaurant. Answer the phone and make excuses why the pizza has still not been delivered.

Vocabulary and useful expressions

The film 'Food Inc' is an excellent resource for this topic.
Nutrition：营养, vitamins：维生素
Protein：蛋白质, carbs：碳水化合物
Diet：日常饮食
Vegetarian：素食者, vegan：严格的素食主义者
Dairy products：乳制品
Pesticides, insecticide：杀虫剂
Organic：有机的
Antibiotics：抗生素, steroids：类固醇, growth hormones：生长激素
Intensive farming：精耕细作, battery farming：层架式禽饲养法

19 Cooking

Brainstorm Vocabulary

What do you know?

At the beginning of class, think of any vocabulary that you already know along with your classmates. If there is anything you don't know then <u>write it in the space below</u> and practice using it during class. Make sure you understand if it's a noun, verb, adjective or adverb. Make sure your pronunciation is accurate and that you know how to use it in a sentence. Is it formal or informal?

Write new vocabulary and expressions here:

Discussion

1: Can you cook? If not, why not?
What is the best thing you can cook?
If you can't cook talk about your mother or father's best dish.

2: Romantic candle lit dinner for two.
If you were going to cook a romantic candle lit dinner for two, what would it be? What special flavours would you use and why? What would you have for <u>dessert</u>?

3: How do you prepare an onion?
Use sequencing such as 'First, second, next and last'.
Use the vocabulary on the white board for utensils and process.

4: How do you make a delicious chicken and salad sandwich?
Use sequencing such as 'First, second, next and last'.
Remember that this should be a <u>delicious</u> sandwich. You should use the flavour list on the white board.

Devil's Advocate

A: Microwave cooking is not real cooking.

B: Cooking is an essential skill that should be taught in middle school.

Role Play

Celebrity Chef
Work in groups of three, though in pairs is also ok.
<u>Person A:</u> You are a famous celebrity chef in China.
Everyone has heard about your cooking.
You have written your own cook books and have your own TV show.
Even Xi Jinping and his wife Peng Liyuan love your cooking and often ask you to cook for them.

Talk about why your food is so popular on CCTV.
What are some of your special recipes and what special flavours do you use?

Person B/C: CCTV interviewer(s).
This is very exciting.
Continually ask follow up questions.
Where do they get their ingredients from?
Where did they get their recipes from?
Why did they want to be a chef?
Are there any other famous people they cook for?
What is Xi Jinping and Peng Liyuan's favourite dish? Why?

Finish Class

Vocabulary and useful expressions

Ingredients: aubergine (UK), eggplant (US): 茄子 salad：沙拉
Cooking oil: sunflower：葵花籽油, olive：橄榄油, soya：大豆油,
peanut oil and lard：花生油和猪油

Flavour ingredients: sugar：糖, salt：盐, vinegar：醋, soy sauce：酱油, lemon
juice：柠檬汁, wine：葡萄酒, beer "啤酒, herbs：香草, curry powder：咖喱粉, red
chillies：红辣椒, black pepper：黑胡椒, garlic：大蒜, ginger：生姜, butter：黄油,
cheese：奶酪

Utensils: Pots and pans：壶和平底锅, steamer：蒸锅, knife：刀, fork：餐叉, spoon：
勺子, chopsticks ('kuaizi' in Pinyin) 筷子, spatula：铲, chopping board：切菜板,
peeler：削皮器

Process: wash：冲洗, clean：清洁, chop：剁, dice：将…切成丁, slice：切片,
cut：切, fry：油炸（煎）, stir-fry：用旺火炒, roast：烘烤, bake,：烘焙 boil：煮沸,
steam：蒸, simmer：炖, toast：烘烤（面包片等） grill：烧烤
Recipe：食谱

20 Eating Out

Brainstorm Vocabulary

What do you know?

At the beginning of class, think of any vocabulary that you already know along with your classmates. If there is anything you don't know then <u>write it in the space below</u> and practice using it during class. Make sure you understand if it is a noun, verb, adjective or adverb. Make sure your pronunciation is accurate and that you know how to use it in a sentence. Is it formal or informal?

Write new vocabulary and expressions here:

Discussion

1: International Cuisine
If you could choose any restaurant from around the world to eat in tonight which one would it be and why? Students are not allowed to choose Chinese food.
Think of six key words for it for, example, Japanese cuisine: *Sushi, miso soup, okayu (porridge), wasabi (horse radish), whale and dolphin.*

2: Service
Give three or four examples of good and bad service in a restaurant.

3: Recommend a great restaurant
What kind of food is it? Where is it? What is the service like? When did you last go?

4: How do you like your tea/coffee?
In England tea is the most common drink. In America it's coffee.
It's very important to make it correctly for people, especially for your boss, clients or if you have guests.
You should ask "How do you take it?" or "How do you like it?"
This means white or black? Sugar or no sugar? How many sugars? People use sugar cubes or a tea spoon to measure.

5: Delicacy
Think of one or two delicacies from around the world, for example, Koreans and Chinese people in the far north like eating dog, in France people like frog's legs and snails.
Is there any food you would not eat? Why?

6: Four course meal
What do we call each part of a four course meal? Write them below with examples of each one:
1:
2:
3:
4:

7: Etiquette
Think of examples of good and bad table manners (in China and Western countries).

Devil's Advocate

McDonalds and KFC are not 'real' restaurants.

126

Role Play

Order food in a restaurant
Part 1:
Person A: Waiter or waitress. Welcome your customers. Use Sir or Madame and be as polite as possible. Recommend the Chef's Special. Take their order
Persons B, C & D: Customers. Order drinks and an entrée.

Part 2:
Customers use the Wonderful Food Menu (see below)
Persons B, C & D: Customers. That food was wonderful. Give lots of praise to the waiter. Be really enthusiastic.
Person A: Waiter or waitress. Greatly accept the praise and tell them why the food is so good.

Finish Class

Vocabulary and useful expressions

Cuisine：烹饪
Italian: spaghetti：意大利面, salami：意大利腊肠,
Mozzarella：意大利干酪（色白味淡）
Service：服务
Mug：马克杯, white/black tea or coffee：加牛奶的茶或者咖啡/红茶或者黑咖啡
Delicacy：美味佳肴
Etiquette：礼仪, table manners：餐桌礼仪
Slurping：大声地啜;出声地喝, chomping：大声地咬，嚼得很响
Four course meal, (appetizer/starter, salad, entrée, dessert) 西餐中四道菜（开胃菜、沙拉、主菜、甜点）
Chef's special：主厨特餐

Wonderful Food Menu

Delicious

A joy   there was so much

The dessert was mouth watering

Heavenly   **Yummy**

Extremely flavourful

Wonderful service – So friendly

I couldn't stop eating

My compliments to the chef

The starter was so fresh

The meat melted in your mouth

Really great   juicy

I'll definitely be coming back again

I would like to leave a huge tip

I just love it here so much

I will tell ALL of my friends

Perfect   Really special

Appendix A

Grammar at a Glance

Article:

Definite Article: *the* is used to restrict the meaning of a noun and give us information about it **Indefinite Article:** a determiner that expresses non-specific reference, such as *a, an,* or *some*

Preposition:
used before <u>nouns</u>, pronouns, or other substantives to form <u>phrases</u> functioning as modifiers of <u>verbs</u>, nouns, or <u>adjectives</u>, and that typically express a spatial, temporal, or other relationship, **as in, on, by, to, since, at, of, off, with.**

A <u>part of speech</u> that indicates the relationship, often spatial, of one word to another, for example, 'She paused <u>at</u> the door', 'This apple is ripe <u>for</u> picking'; and 'They talked the matter over face <u>to</u> face.' Some common prepositions are *at, by, for, from, in, into, on, to,* **and** *with.*

Noun:
Nouns are a class of words that are subjects of verbs and prepositions. They can be used in plurals. Nouns often refer to people, places, things, states and quantities.

Subject Pronoun:
What are <u>you</u> looking at? e.g. **I, me, you, him, he, she, this, who, what** takes the place of a noun.

Verb:
Verbs are used to describe actions, states and relationships between two or more things.

Adjective:
Adjectives describe and modify nouns or pronouns. They can be before such as the red car or after such as the car is red.

Adverb: Adverbs are used to modify a **verb, an adjective, or another adverb**:

> 1: Mary sings *terribly*
> 2: David is *extremely* stupid
> 3: This car goes *incredibly* slow

In 1, the adverb *beautifully* tells us how Mary sings. In 2, *extremely* tells us the degree to which David is stupid. Finally, in 3, the adverb *incredibly* tells us how slowly the car goes.

Many adverbs end in ly e.g. slowly, quickly, softly, suddenly, and gradually
> Adjectives: slow, quick, soft, sudden, gradual

Adverbs are gradable e.g. soft = very softly, extremely quickly, really gently
These modifying words are also adverbs and called **Degree Adverbs**
(almost, barely, entirely, highly, quite, slightly, totally, and utterly)

Comparative Adverbs: use more e.g. more recently, more frequently
Superlative Adverbs: use most e.g. most recently, most frequently

Adverbs do not modify nouns.

Phrasal Verbs: When a verb is added to a preposition or adverb the meaning of the verb changes, for example, 'My car broke down last night' > break down. Phrasal verbs can have more than one meaning. In this case someone who is upset can break down.
There are around 3,000 phrasal verbs. They are impossible to quantify due to informal and formal usage.

Some are **separable** and can be split up and still form a sentence:
'Take off your coat' > 'Take your coat off.'
'She looked up the word' > 'She looked the word up'
'He ate up all his dinner' >'He ate all his dinner up'.

Some are **inseparable**
'We are looking into the problem.' (would be *looking the problem into*)
'Look after the children.' (would be *look the children after*)
'I called on a friend' (would be I called a friend on)

Predicate: Every complete sentence contains two parts: a **subject** and a **predicate**. The subject is what (or whom) the sentence is about, while the predicate tells something about the subject. In the following sentences, the predicate is placed in brackets ( ), while the subject is highlighted.

> **Barry** (runs).
> **Barry and his dog** (run on the hill every morning).

Coordinating Conjunction: join or link words or phrases together within a sentence. Some coordinating conjunctions are **and, yet, for, and but.**

Subordinating Conjunctions: are found at the beginning of independent clauses. Some common subordinating conjunctions are **if, although, since and while.**

Demonstrative Determiner: used to demonstrate the identity of the thing referenced by the following noun; in English, they include **this, these, that and those** e.g. 'I like this dictionary' the word 'this' is a demonstrative determiner.

Clause: is a group of words which act as a single unit and is built round a verb, for example, 'he lives in the UK'

Compound and complex sentences contain two or more clauses:

Simple: 'Barry is living in the UK'.

Compound: 'He lives in the UK, but his family is still in China'.

Complex: 'While his family is still in China, Barry is staying with friends'.

Relative Clauses: A sentence or statement that can give extra information.
They can bring two parts of a sentence together to make dialogue more fluent.
To do this we use **relative pronouns,** for example, 'A girl is talking to Tom. Do you know the girl?'>'Do you know the girl who is talking to Tom?'

- **That:** Subject or Object pronoun for people, animals or things
- **Who:** Subject or Object for people
- **Which:** Subject or Object for animals or things
- **Which:** Referring to a whole sentence, for example, 'He couldn't say the letter T which surprised me'.
- **Whose:** Possession for animals or things

If Clauses: There are three types of conditional if-clauses
- Conditional Sentence 1: Here it is possible and also very probable that the condition will be completed:
Form: If + simple present = will (future)
E.g.: If I see his wife, Ill tell her he's down the bar.
- Conditional Sentence 2: Here it is possible but unlikely, that the condition will be completed.
Form: If + simple past = conditional (would + infinitive)
E.g.: If I saw his wife, I would tell her he was down the bar.

- Conditional Sentence 3: Here it is impossible that the condition will be completed because it is referring to the past.
Form: If + past perfect = conditional (would have + past participle)
Example: If I had seen his wife, I would have told her he was down the bar.

3rd Person – Simple present tense: he, she, them and they
'Joe walks down the street with his hands in his pockets'.
'She stares into the mirror at the failure before her'.
- **He/She**: Third person singular
- **It:** Third person singular
- **They**: Third person plural

2nd Person – Simple present tense: You stare into the mirror at the failure before you.
- **You**: Second person singular

1st Person – Simple present tense: I stare into the mirror at the failure before me 1st
- **I**: First person singular
- **We**: First person plural

VERB FORMS

Lexical Verb: contain some sort of meaning and can stand alone, e.g. 'I love chocolate'

Auxiliary Verb: 1: help the lexical verb e.g. 'He's watching TV' = 'is'
      2: to make the sentence 'He lives here' negative, add does to make 'He doesn't live here'
      3: to create a question 'Does he live here?'
Remember: **be, do and have** can function in different forms.
Remember: be has different present and past forms: am, are is, has and were
However, all three can be used as lexical and auxiliary verbs as well e.g.
'I didn't arrive on time' + auxiliary
'I did my homework' = lexical only

Modal Auxiliary Verbs: carry meaning: can, could, may, might, will, would, shall, should, must, need, ought to and dare e.g. 'I must go'.

Base Form of a verb: e.g. 'He listens' the base form is to listen.

Present Participle ends in 'ing'. Are verb forms used to function as an adjective.
They are the only verb forms that stay completely regular (see below).

The present participle is used with an auxiliary to express the progressive aspect (see below)
'That film is very exciting'

Past Participle ends in 'ed' or 'en' and it has two functions:

1) Adjective

E.g.: This car **is** <u>heated</u>. (Verb: 'is'; Adjective 'heated')
E.g.: We had **a** <u>heated</u> discussion. (Adjective 'heated')
E.g.: I had seen it, I have seen it, I will have seen it, It was seen

As an adjective, the past participle occurs after the verb **BE** (is, am, was, were, been) or it modifies a noun.

2) As part of a verb

E.g.: The stove **has** <u>heated</u> the room. (Verb: 'has'; Part of a verb: 'heated')

As a part of a verb, the past participle occurs with the verb **HAVE** (have, has, had).

Gerunds: verb + ing 'I'm working as hard as I can' or 'Running is good for your health'
They are only formed with the infinitive + ing
Note the difference between a progressive which uses is was has have would etc
Gerund: A verb form with 'ing' forming a noun, for example, 'I am going <u>running</u>'.

S-Forms: she plays, he works

Ing-Forms: playing, running

Finite Verbs: form the main part of a sentence. Non-finite is therefore an infinitive, gerund or participle

Infinitives: Verbs that have to before them. Sometimes they will be no to but the verb still remains the infinitive such as feel, hear, help, make, let, see and watch.

Action Verbs/State Verbs: 'Nigel went to school' = action. 'I'm buying a new car' = action
                              'Nigel was busy' = state. 'I need a new car' = state
'Action' is something happening e.g. do, go buy, play stop, take
'State' is something staying the same e.g. be, doubt, believe, know, want, seem

Regulars Verbs: Most verbs are regular. If we add 'ed' to them to put them into the past, the spelling or pronunciation is the same. 'I walked' can be used in past tense or past participle,
'I walked', 'I have walked'

Irregular Verbs: (around 400) Their sound or spelling changes when we put them into the past, for example, 'make = made', 'give = gave(s) or given (pp)', 'saw = seen'
Was, bite, bring, break, bought, and began
Some irregular verbs are the same in past simple and past participle e.g. make/made/made

Mixing different verb forms to create phrases:
1. e.g. Combine irregular v 'have' as an auxiliary to the **– ing** lexical 'be'
'I have been'
2. e.g. combine modal 'should' with base form 'have' and past participle of 'study'
'I should have studied'

Past Tense refers to a verb, (remember that past participles are not verbs.)

E.g.: The stove <u>heated</u> the room.
E.g.: I saw it

In the example above, the word heated doesnt do the following things:

It doesn't occur with BE (is, am, was, were, been)
It doesn't occur with HAVE (have, has, have)
It doesnt modify a noun (argument)

'heated' functions all by itself. It's a verb, and the 'ed' ending tells us it's a past tense verb

Present Perfect: Actually still refers to a past event: We use the Present Perfect to say that an action happened at an unspecified time before now. The exact time is not important. You CANNOT use the Present Perfect with specific time expressions such as: yesterday, one year ago, last week, when I was a child, when I lived in China, at that moment, that day, one day, etc. We CAN use the Present Perfect with unspecific expressions such as: ever, never, once, many times, several times, before, so far, already, yet, etc.
Present Perfect examples:
I **have seen** that film twenty times.
I think I **have met** him once before.
There **have been** many earthquakes in Japan.
People **have travelled** to the Moon.
People **have not travelled** to Jupiter.
Have you **read** the book yet?
Nobody **has** ever **climbed** that mountain.

A: **Has** there ever **been** a war in Europe?
B: Yes, there **has been** a war in the Europe.

Past Perfect: The Past Perfect expresses the idea that something occurred before
another action in the past. It can also show that something happened before a specific
time in the past.
I **had** never **seen** such a beautiful beach before I went to Kauai.
I did not have any money because I **had lost** my wallet.
Tony knew Istanbul so well because he **had visited** the city several times.

Future perfect: The Future Perfect expresses the idea that something will occur
before another action in the future. It can also show that something will happen before a
specific time in the future.
By next November, I **will have received** my promotion.
By the time he *gets* home, she **is going to have cleaned** the entire house.
I **am not going to have finished** this test by 3 o'clock.

Progressive Aspect: also called Continuous uses 'to be'

A. Present progressive = am + (base form + -ing): I am working OR is + (base form + -
ing):
She is eating. OR are + (base form + -ing): We are studying.

1. A planned activity: Sofia is starting school at CEC tomorrow

2. An activity that is occurring right now: Jan is watching TV right now.

3. An activity that is in progress, although not actually occurring at the time of speaking:
Sara is learning English at CEC.

B. Past progressive = was + (base form + -ing): I was working. OR were + (base form
+ -ing): They were eating.

1. A past activity in progress while another activity occurred: At 6:00 yesterday I was
eating dinner. The phone rang while I was eating.

2. Two past activities in progress at the same time: While I was answering the phone, my
wife was cooking dinner.

C. Future progressive = will be + (base form + -ing): I will be working. He will be
eating.

An activity that will be in progress: This time next year we will be living in Canada.

We can also ask about someone's plans using the future progressive.
Will you be going to Canada next year?

D. Present perfect progressive = have + (base form + -ing): I have been working. OR has + (base form + -ing): She has been eating.

1. This tense emphasizes the duration of an activity that began in the past and continues into the present. It often uses time words or phrases. It may be used to refer to continuing activity that is recent: He has been painting houses all summer. I've been studying English for 2 years.

2. It may be used to refer to continuing activity that is recent: He has been going to school at CEC.

E. Past perfect progressive = had + (base form + -ing): I had been working. He had been eating.

When the teacher arrived, I had been waiting almost 10 minutes. He was out of breath because he had been running to catch the bus.

F. Future perfect progressive = will have + (base form + -ing): I will have been working. She will have been eating. This tense emphasizes the duration of a continuing activity in the future that ends before another activity or time in the future.

By 2003 Janet will have been studying English at CEC for 3 years. By 9:45 tonight I will have been sitting in class for 2 hours and 45 minutes.

Active Verbs (voice): In active sentences, the thing doing the action is the subject of the sentence and the thing receiving the action is the object. Most sentences we say are active.

(Thing doing action) + (verb) + (thing receiving action)

The teacher (subject) teaches (active verb) the students (object)
Students (subject) do (active verb) their homework (object)

Passive Verbs (voice): In passive sentences, the thing receiving the action is the subject of the sentence and the thing doing the action is optionally included near the end of the sentence.

(Thing receiving action) + (be) + (past participle of verb) + (by) + (thing doing action)

The students (sub) are taught (passive verb) by the teacher (object)
Homework (sub) is done (passive verb) by the students (object)

Appendix B

Using Phonetics

A basic knowledge of phonetics is very useful and most Chinese students use it as a guide in their pronunciation. Write the relevant symbol under new vocabulary if you are having problems with pronunciation. The various symbols plus examples are below. The sounds where students have the most frequent difficulties are interlined.

Iː fleece	I minute	ʊ foot	uː group	Iə near	eI face	
e head	ə common	3ː nurse	ɔː thought	ʊə store	ɔI choice	əʊ show
æ track	ʌ love	ɑː start	ɒ lot	eə fair	ɑI high	ɑʊ round
p plant	b black	t trust	d ladder	tʃ church	dʒ judge	k key	g get
f future	v heavy	θ thank	ð this	s soon	z zoo	ʃ ship	ʒ usual
m mountain	n Nigeria	ŋ king	h heavy	l valley	r robin	w windy	j useful

Consonants

p: pen, copy, happen
b: back, baby, job
t: tea, tight, button
d: day, ladder, odd
k: key, clock, school
g: get, giggle, ghost
tʃ: church, match, nature
dʒ: judge, age, soldier
f: fat, coffee, rough, photo
v: view, heavy, move
θ: thing, author, path
ð: this, other, smooth
s: soon, cease, sister
z: zero, music, roses, buzz
ʃ: ship, sure, national
ʒ: pleasure, vision
h: hot, whole, ahead
m: more, hammer, sum
n: nice, know, funny, sun
ŋ: ring, anger, thanks, sung
l: light, valley, feel
r: right, wrong, sorry, arrange
j: use, beauty, few
w: wet, one, when, queen
ʔ: (glottal stop)department, football
(often used in the UK)

Vowels

ɪ : kit, bid, hymn, minute
e: dress, bed, head, many
æ: trap, bad
ɒ: lot, odd, wash
ʌ: strut, mud, love, blood
ʊ: foot, good, put
ɪ : : fleece, sea, machine
eɪ: face, day, break
aɪ: price, high, try
ɔɪ: choice, boy
u : : goose, two, blue, group
əʊ: goat, show, no
aʊ: mouth, now, brown
ɪə: near, here, weary
eə: square. fair, various
ɑ : : start, father
ɔ : : thought, law, north, war
ʊə: poor, jury, cure
ɜ : nurse, stir, learn, refer
ə: about, common, standard
i: happy, radiate. glorious
u: thank you, influence, situation

138

www.ingramcontent.com/pod-product-compliance
Lightning Source LLC
Chambersburg PA
CBHW081212020426
42331CB00012B/3006